A Taste of Love from the Heart,

with love Nanie

Angel Baby Press
3127 W. Vuelta De Los Mineros
Tucson, AZ 85745

Interior Book Layout: The Printed Page, Phoenix, AZ

To love life and love others, one has to have a clean spirit and honest mind — respect for yourself and respect for others will bring your soul peace and harmony!

— Barbara Carrillo

About the Author

A true native of Tucson, Barbara A. Carrillo was born and raised in the Old Pueblo. She started her career in the Missile Defense industry at the ripe age of seventeen. After graduating from high school, she was determined to continue her education and advance in her career. Barbara and her husband David were married in Tucson, Arizona in October of 1973. They both continued working and planning for their future. Two years later, in September of 1975, they were the proud parents of their first beautiful son, Jody. Barbara stayed home for fifteen months to be with her son and shortly after returned to work for approximately one year. In August of 1978, Barbara and David gave birth to their second beautiful son, Jimmy.

As life and dreams do not always turn out the way we plan, Barbara and David divorced in 1986. Barbara continued her responsibility as a mother, with this being her number one focus in life. With determination and perseverance, she went on to continue her career and education. Barbara received a dual Bachelor's degree in Business and Management and a Master's degree in Organizational Management. Working numerous professions throughout her career in missile defense, she discovered her strength and enthusiasm in Marketing and Communications. Indeed, with her talents and efforts she was able to utilize her creativity and writing skills to accomplish her objective.

In Barbara's free time, she devoted many hours volunteering time in the community. She developed an extreme passion for her Hispanic culture. In 1982, she became one of the original founders of her company's Hispanic Employee's Association.

Enthusiastic to launch this organization, Barbara volunteered to serve on the board and on various committees until she retired in 2005.

But, life and work do not end just because you retire, as a retiree; they still keep her informed and invite her to participate in various events. Also, Barbara is still utilizing her skills and talents working out of her home and pursuing her writing. The difference is there are no deadlines, personalities and behavioral characteristics that she has to accommodate. Life is good!

Acknowledgments

Today is December 1, 2006, and as I begin writing my book, I would like to honor and pay tribute to my father Pedro Audelio Carrillo who died on this day fourteen years ago. I miss you Dad, and wish you were here with us, but I know your spirit is always in our presence.

I want to thank my mother Anita Avila Carrillo who has shown me the basics of cooking and has shared many of her own recipes and those from her mother, Anna Serna Avila, and my father's mother, Rita Valenzuela Carrillo. I was also fortunate to have the honor to meet my great-grandmother, Carolina Branche Serna, my mother's grandmother, which also contributed to the traditions of many of these legacies.

I have altered many of these recipes to be quick and easy to prepare, but yet to still retain the same great taste and flavor. Please note that I have added or deleted ingredients that were desirable to my own taste. So, do not take offense to the modifications that I have taken to amend these recipes. Several recipes are my own creations that I have experimented with and have let my imagination run free.

To my sons Jody and Jimmy thank you so much for all the happiness that you have brought in my life. I am so proud of both of you; and know that I have been blessed to be able to witness you becoming the gentlemen that I had envisioned you would become. A big thank you to my daughter-in-law's for your part in the creation of my beautiful precious grandchildren. To the father of my children, thank you, David, for the beautiful sons we conceived together. What a miraculous gift to watch our sons continuing the family tree as they bear our beautiful grandchildren. And to you, my grandbabies, know that you will always be my treasured little angels and that you have brought Nanie so much joy into her life. I ask God to keep his angel's wings around you at all times and keep you safe from any harm. As I compose this book, I leave with you my love and memories of recipes that have been carried down through the generations.

To my family and friends who have encouraged me to go forward with my endeavor and have possibly shared with me your own recipes, although many of them I have changed, in various ways, they still provide a link to my accomplishment. I want to express my appreciation to all of you, for your support and confidence in me (you know who you are).

My deepest gratitude and admiration to Styne Hill, my friend, my co-worker, my boss and my mentor. Thank you so much for the beautiful silver-plated mouse you surprised me with at my retirement party, September 1, 2005; it has already been put to great use compiling this book. I enjoyed the years I worked with you and the pillar of trust that you exhibited in me; this I will always cherish.

I would like to give special thanks to my editor and publishing consultant, Jan McCracken. I appreciate you sharing your knowledge with me and helping me through the tough hurdles.

To my layout and book designer, Lisa Liddy—we did it! Thank you for your patience and expertise in completing this book. My deepest gratitude to you for your kindness and understanding through this project!

Susan Encinas, my web designer, longtime friend and coworker, I can't thank you enough for your creativity/enthusiasm in bringing my vision to life. Not only are you a dynamic person, but your work is fantastic—you are the best!

I look forward to working with all of you on my next book.

Dedication

I dedicate this book to my two adoring sons, Joseph Larry Gamboa (Jody) and James Christopher Gamboa (Jimmy). May you continue these traditions and enjoy creating your own. I leave you this book with love and devotion, with the wish that you will pass it down to all my grandchildren to continue this legacy.

Joseph L. Gamboa and James C. Gamboa
Photo taken at the Tanque Verde Guest Ranch —
previously named "La Cebadilla Ranch"
Tata was so proud of you...

Preface

Many folks use various treatments, medications and therapy for relieving stress... my cure was cooking! I realized that when I began cooking, my mind was free of troubles and the stress seemed to be reduced. The excitement of creating and producing an attractive and superb food masterpiece is a rewarding passion that surpasses all stress.

As years have gone by, I have passed down the love, magic and passion for cooking to my sons. This in itself is so gratifying. Watching the joy they experience in cooking for family and friends is truly a blessing. For me, it is such an honor when my sons call me and ask how to make an entree or need a recipe for a special dish.

My hope is that this book will serve as confirmation that if you have a desire to do something, you can. Anyone can cook if they want to, but for those who have a passion for this so called art, the secret is to let your creativity and confidence run free. As I always expressed to my sons when they were growing up, "you can do anything you want to, if you put your mind to it"; and "if you are going to do something, do it right." This was repeatedly stated to me by my father as I was growing up.

The recipes I have chosen to include in this book to share with you, symbolize foods connected to many of my childhood memories and traditions. Many of the recipes represent my Mexican-American heritage. I am very proud to be part of such a beautiful and unique culture.

Introduction

As I begin to describe to you the various recipes and where many of them originated, I will share with you some of the cultural history of the Arizona Territory that both my parents, aunts, uncles and cousins shared with me.

After the signing of the Gadsden Purchase Peace Treaty with Mexico in 1853, many cattlemen, soldiers, miners and adventurous men and women migrated to the Arizona Territory to claim their fortunes. Mercantile stores, business firms, homes and schools were booming. These settlers brought growth to the Old Pueblo of Tucson and for that we owe thanks to our Mexican ancestors.

My father, Pedro Audelio Carrillo, was a third generation Tucsonian pioneer rancher whose family helped develop the cattle industry in southeastern Arizona in 1877. His grandfather, Don Emilio Carrillo, came from Sonora, Mexico in 1854. Several years later he met his bride, Catalina Elias. Conserving his savings, Don Emilio urbanized the Buena Vista Ranch, which was later renamed La Cebadilla Ranch. The ranch is located at the foothills of the Rincon Mountains just east of Tucson.

Don Emilio Carrillo was very well known in Tucson and recognized as a fine cattleman. His brand was known as Los Gonchos.

Bandits, who claimed he had hidden treasures of gold, hung him from the beams of La Cebadilla Ranch in his own living room. He refused to reveal to them where he had his money hidden, and they left him hanging to die. Sadly, he died four years later, from complications resulting from the trauma. When Don Emilio died on February 14, 1908, the ranch was acquired by his oldest son, my grandfather, Rafael Carrillo. Grandfather changed the brand of the ranch to "RC (Rafael Carrillo)."

Today this ranch is known as the Tanque Verde Guest Ranch. The original building materials of adobe brick for walls, native stone for fireplace, mesquite and saguaro ribs for ceiling still remain, as well as many pieces of the furniture and some of the walls are marked with this famous brand.

After Dad's passing I talked with his youngest sister, Aunt Alice, and asked her about her childhood upbringing and about my grandmother, Rita Carrillo. I remember staying up till 2:00 a.m. on her porch in Cholla Bay, Mexico, intently listening to stories about the Carrillo's and life on the ranch. She recollected her school years and talked about their home in town where they lived during the week so the children could attend school. I remember this home quite well. It was so quaint and full of history. I can see the beautiful wood floors, built-in mirrored china cabinets, shelves built into the walls and a spooky outside cellar. There was a big living room window facing the University of Arizona stadium, on the Southeast corner of Sixth Street and Warren in Tucson, Arizona. The property was eventually sold to the university and transformed into a student parking lot.

I wanted to know the secrets of my Grandma Carrillo's green corn tamales. Aunt Alice recalls the long drive to the ranch when the children accompanied Grandma during the weekends. The hot summertime during June, July and August was tamale season. This was the time to clean the white corn and prepare the green corn tamales. Aunt Alice stated, "green corn tamales were the worst to make and she was a tough one." Each kernel of corn had to be removed by hand, without using knives or any kitchen tools. There would be no waste!

I also remember visiting with Aunt Mary, Dad's middle sister and Uncle Goodman his brother-in-law, in Saint David, Arizona and getting the recipe for "Grandma Carrillo's Salsa." Garlic was and still is, the key to great recipes! Aunt Leanor, Dad's oldest sister, was also a great cook and such a fine lady. She was famous for her Viscochuelo cookies.

Introduction

The family took great pride in running the ranch but as years went by, Grandfather was stricken with diabetes and died at an early age of fifty-two. The distance to the ranch became overwhelming and extreme as well as the cost of up keep became impossible. Grandma, Rita V. Carrillo, decided to place the ranch up for sale. Dad told me that this made him very sad as he was only seventeen when his father died, but he also knew what a great hardship this was for Grandma. When Grandfather died, it was like the ranch died with him.

Dad was so very proud of his childhood memories and he shared many stories with me a month before his passing. He shared the pain of his father dying. He said that it hurt so much and he never wanted his children to feel the pain he felt.

Dad was now seventy-seven and I knew he was preparing me - I could see the sadness in his eyes. I was biting my tongue and holding back the tears. I left Dad's and cried all the way home. I remember sharing with my sons the sadness that I felt. On Thanksgiving Day, two days before he left us, he sat down next to me on the couch and said, "'mija' (my daughter) you can see and feel when someone is not well can't you?" Yes, I could! I could see it in his eyes and it hurt so, so very much. My heart ached with pain to see my father's sadness. I felt like my world came to an end when he passed away, but his spirit gave me the strength to carry on his memory. As I write this book, I cherish those memories and talks that we shared together. He will forever remain in my heart.

Time has passed and the pain and grief has healed within. Talking with my sons, my family and friends helped immensely to mend the wounds. We all share grief in different degrees and no one person can measure our pain. I still get teary eyed with certain songs, pictures, dates and certain holidays, but this only means that my love is still so very strong and will never ever die. I will always honor and hold the deepest and sincere admiration for my parents and ancestors and it is my hope that I have instilled this worthy value in my own children.

In memory of my Father

Pedro Audelio (Pete) Carrillo
Born 7-2-1915 - 12-1-1992

Don Emilio Carrillo –
Great Grandfather
1841–1908

Rita Valenzuela Carrillo
Grandmother
1888–1980

Rafael Carrillo
Grandfather
1882 -1932

Dad's days at the ranch rustling the cows...
"La Cebadilla Ranch" now known as the
Tanque Verde Guest Ranch

Pedro Audelio Carrillo

Dad and Mom at "La Cebadilla Ranch"
horseback riding

*Pedro Audelio Carrillo
and Anita Avila Carrillo*

Introduction

Mrs. De Serna Dies At 106 In Nogales

The widow of a former governor of Sonora, Mex., and grandmother of the wife of the present governor, died Sunday in Nogales, Son., at the age of 106.

Mrs. Carolina Vda. de Serna, widow of Gen. Francisco de Serna who served as governor in the late 1800s, died at the home of a daughter, Mrs. Maclovia Vda. de Lujan. Gen. de Serna died in 1895.

Among Mrs. de Serna's 234 descendants is Mrs. Luis Encinas, of Hermosillo, Son., wife of the present governor of Sonora.

Other survivors include four other daughters, Mrs. Otillia Vda. de Celaya, also of Nogales; Mrs. Adelaida Vda. de Trelles and Mrs. Isabel Vda. de Gonzales, both of Hermosillo, and Mrs. Ana Vda. de Avila, of Tucson.

Forty-two of Mrs. de Serna's 51 great-great-grandchildren live in Tucson.

In 1961, my great grandmother on my mother's side of the family, Carolina Branche Serna, peacefully passed away in Nogales, Sonora, Mexico at the age of 106 years! Most of her extended family members referred to her as Mama Calina. She was born in the small town of Choix, Sinaloa, Mexico and lived there until the age of five. She was, then raised in the town of Alamos, Sonora, Mexico where she met her husband General Francisco Serna. They eventually relocated to Santa Anna, Sonora, Mexico and in due time gave birth to five daughters - Maclovia Lujan, Maria Anna Serna Avila, Otilla Celaya, Adelida Trellez and Isabel Gonzales. She was widowed at a young age and began experiencing serious health problems. The family discussed her condition and they agreed that it would be best for her to sell her home and rotate visits among the daughters. She ultimately settled in Nogales, Arizona for the remainder of her life. I remember visiting her and the wonderful hospitality we received from her siblings. She was highly regarded with honor and respect from all family members.

Being still very young, I saw Ma Calina as a small, kind and gentle woman that always greeted you with a smile and respect. Some of the family members remember vividly her visits that she made to Tucson and her innovative creations that she completed during her short stay. She would collect old socks from the children and tear them into strips. As the children gathered around her to listen to

Introduction

stories of per past, she would be producing two or three rugs to leave for the family.

Ma Calina left many of her recipes to her five daughters, one being my grandmother, Maria Anna Serna Avila. Grandma Avila was referred to as the strong and resilient daughter of the family. She met my grandfather, Enrique Avila, in Santa Anna, Sonora, Mexico. On September 13, 1900, the two exchanged their wedding vows. Grandfather had previously been residing in Santa Clara, California, where he had been attending college and graduated from the University of Santa Clara. He worked for several years as a mining prospector in Mexico.

After their marriage, he became mayor of Hermosillo, Sonora, Mexico. He sent an urgent message to Grandma expressing the severity of the revolution indicating that she needed to move herself and the children to safety. In November of 1914 and with the help of a friend and other siblings, she moved her children Carlos, Bernardo, Belem, Carolina, Maria Jesus, Oscar and Florencio from Santa Anna, Mexico to Tucson, Arizona to establish a new life for her family. Two years later, Grandma gave birth to her seventh child, my mother, Anita. More children followed — Enrique, Adeline and Maria Teresa. My grandfather spent much of his time in Sonora and Grandma ultimately raised her ten children on her own with help from her sons. She was able to provide a safe and secure life for her children.

A strong lady and deserving of the respect she received by all, she is to be commended and honored for her loyalty and perseverance to her offspring.

Not only did she raise her ten children and three grandchildren, but she opened her heart and home to Florencio, a young seven year old Yaqui boy who was abandoned at the train station in Hermosillo, Mexico. At that time, in the early 1900's, many families fled to the Yucatan and were separated from their loved ones. Florencio lived with Grandma until he was a grown man. Sadly, she

Introduction

received word that a body of a young man in his early thirties was found on the railroad tracks, believing to be Florencio, so she went to the authorities to identify the body. Yes, it was Florencio; he was left on the railroad track after being murdered to make it look like he had been run over by a train. The county helped with the funeral expenses, so with dignity, he was given a proper funeral and the Avila family was named as his siblings.

My parent's lived two blocks from Aunt Adeline and Uncle Henry's home, where Grandma resided. So, during my youthful years, I remember going over to stay with Grandma after school when Mom was not home. The wonderful fragrance of beans warming in the oven, gordita tortillas on the stove or hamburger and potatoes tacos being prepared, leaves me with such heart felt memories. The ultimate was Christmas — it stood out from all other occasions. It was tradition that everyone stopped over to visit and pay their respects to Grandma. But, the most memorable impression of my childhood was the simplicity and the invaluable gift of everyone enjoying each other... not to mention the aroma of red chili tamales hot off the stove.

On August 1, 1968, Grandma passed away, after battling cancer. How magnificent that Grandma's mother was able to see her daughter mature to the age of seventy eight years. Although "Grandma Avila" is not physically with us, she left behind a legacy of strength and honor for all her ancestors to learn and pursue.

My thanks to my mother

Anita Avila Carrillo
Born 1-15-1916

Dona Carolina Branche Serna
Great Grandmother
1854 – 1961

Anna Serna Avila
Grandmother
1883 – 1968

Enrique Serrano Avila
Grandfather
1873 -1937

Contents

A Taste of Love from the Heart

A Taste of Love from the Heart

A Taste of Love from the Heart

A Taste of Love from the Heart

A Taste of Love from the Heart

A Taste of Love from the Heart

Barbara's Favorite Name Brands and Tortilla Factories

Through the years of cooking and experimenting with food brands and food factories, I discovered that some brands absolutely worked better for me than others. Here is a list that I would like to share with you of my preferences of ingredients that I use for recipes in this book. Some ingredients such as flour for tortillas give the masa (dough) a nice soft, yet workable texture to strength the tortillas so they are nice and thin. Also, some brands contain ingredients in them that may taste better or create a magic in the food.

- ▲ Albers Corn Meal
- ▲ Best Food Mayonnaise
- ▲ Clamato Tomato Juice
- ▲ Crisco Shortening
- ▲ Grand Tortilla Factory in Tucson, AZ (they stone grind the corn)
- ▲ Hershey's Cocoa
- ▲ Jell-O Desserts
- ▲ Karo Corn Syrup
- ▲ Knorr - Caldo De Tomate and Caldo De Pollo
- ▲ La Buena Tortilla Factory in Tucson, AZ
  (they make thin corn tortillas for crispy tacos)
- ▲ La Pina Flour
- ▲ Lipton Onion Soup
- ▲ Marie Calendar Corn Bread Mix
- ▲ Masterpiece Barbeque Sauce
- ▲ Minute Rice
- ▲ Mrs. Wright's Liquid Smoke
- ▲ Pillsbury Ready Made Pie Crust
- ▲ Ritz Crackers
- ▲ Santa Cruz Chili Paste
- ▲ Splenda Sugar Substitute
- ▲ Tabasco Hot Sauce
- ▲ Uncle Ben's Original Rice
- ▲ V8 Vegetable Juice

All recipes can be reduced in quantity by cutting ingredients equally.

A Taste of Love from the Heart

Notes

Beans

Chili Beans

Ingredients:
5 cups clean pinto beans
3 to 4 quarts of water
1 lb lean hamburger meat
1 tbsp fresh garlic
1 cup diced brown onion
1 small can of tomato sauce
1 cup Santa Cruz Chili paste
Salt/ pepper/garlic salt/
    onion salt to taste

1. Use clean beans in a bag and place in a 5-quart slow cooker.
2. Fill slow cooker almost to the top with water.
3. Cook on high for 1 hour then turn to low for 5 to 6 hours. Beans should be firm enough to hold its shape (not too soft or they will fall apart).
4. In a skillet sauté onion and hamburger meat.
5. Add meat to beans.
6. Add chili paste and tomato sauce.
7. Add salt, pepper, onion salt and garlic salt to taste.

These chili beans are great with homemade yeast bread (see page 169 for yeast bread recipe). I especially liked to prepare this meal during rainy gloomy days. It sure helped to perk up the spirit. This meal is a feast by itself, it is filling and easy to prepare. Wow are those memories and recollections rolling in! Here's to you Mike Gamboa—you loved those chili beans, but yeast bread touched your heart. I cherish those memories that the family spent together. God Bless you till we meet again.

A Taste of Love from the Heart

Smashed beans takes strength in the arms and a powerful grip to continuously pound to a smooth creamy texture. I was very fortunate to have this power tool "Mr. Muscle," he was one of the neighborhood kids that was like a son to me; Cris Romero. He loved smashing the homemade beans and helping me cook. To this day at the age of 31 Cris tells me that he loves going down memory lane and remembering the beans, tortillas, tamales, ribs we grilled outdoors and the Christmas cookies.

My life was so blessed by God to have these fond memories to look back on and to know that my son's lives were filled with values and happy recollections of there childhood upbringing. I loved to grill outdoors and the boys would always have their friends over for a swim and a cookout. Their friends were so considerate and always willing and eager to help out in preparing, picking up or cleaning up the mess.

Little things that we take for granted, such as cooking outdoors, some of the boys friends had never had picnics or cookouts outside with their families, so this was an exciting treat for them.

Not only was Cris a great bean smasher, but he could knead tortilla dough for me in minutes. There was a catch; he loved eating the gordita tortillas hot off the grill with melted butter.

We didn't always have lot of money, but we always had a lot of fun, love and memories that no dollar amount could ever replace. Thank you Cris for being so helpful, you will always be very special to me.

Smashed Pinto Beans

Ingredients:
5 cups clean pinto beans
3 to 4 quarts of water
1/4 cup canola oil
1/2 pound of Quesadilla
   cheese
Salt to taste

1. Use clean beans in a bag and place in a 5-quart slow cooker.
2. Fill slow cooker almost to the top with water and add oil.
3. First slow cooker on high for 1 hour then turn to low for 10 to 11 hours (the secret is the time).
4. Remove from heat.
5. Remove liquid and add as needed after mashing beans.
6. Beans should be creamy (no lumps).
7. Add cheese.
8. Add salt to taste (remember the cheese contains salt).

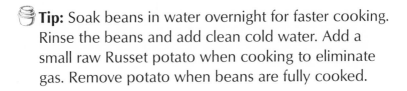 **Tip:** Soak beans in water overnight for faster cooking. Rinse the beans and add clean cold water. Add a small raw Russet potato when cooking to eliminate gas. Remove potato when beans are fully cooked.

Whole Pinto Beans with Green Chili & Bacon

Ingredients:
5 cups clean pinto beans
3 to 4 quarts water
2 small cans diced green chili
2 cups diced small bacon pieces
1 whole garlic head with peeling
1 small whole peeled yellow onion
Salt/garlic salt/onion salt to taste

1. Use clean beans in a bag and place in a 5-quart slow cooker.
2. Fill slow cooker almost to the top with water.
3. Add whole garlic head and yellow onion.
4. Add green chili.
5. Add small pieces of bacon.
6. Cook on high for 1 hour.
7. Reduce heat to low and simmer for 5 to 6 hours (beans should be firm enough to hold their shape, but not too soft or they will fall apart).
8. Remove from heat.
9. Add salt; onion salt and garlic salt to taste.

Whole Pinto Beans with Green Onion & Cheese

Ingredients:
5 cups clean pinto beans
3 to 4 quarts of water
1/2 pound grated Jack cheese
1 cup diced green onions
1/4 cup oregano
Salt/onion salt to taste

1. Use clean beans in a bag and place in a 5-quart slow cooker.

2. Fill slow cooker almost to the top with water.

3. First put slow cooker on high for 1 hour then turn to low for 6 to 8 hours or until beans are firm enough to hold its shape (not too soft or they will fall apart).

4. Remove half of liquid if there is too much (should be soup consistency).

5. Add salt; onion salt to taste and rub hands with oregano; sprinkle.

6. Add green onions and cheese on top of the beans.

Whole Pinto Beans with Red Chili & Bacon

Ingredients:

5 cups clean pinto beans

3 quarts water

1 cup chili paste

2 cups diced small bacon pieces

1 whole garlic head with peeling

1 small whole peeled yellow onion

Salt/garlic salt to taste

1. Use clean beans in a bag and place in a 5-quart slow cooker.

2. Fill slow cooker with 3 quarts water.

3. Add whole garlic head and whole yellow onion.

4. Add red chili paste.

5. Add small pieces of bacon.

6. Cook on high for 1 hour.

7. Reduce heat to low and simmer for 5 to 6 hours (beans should be firm enough to hold their shape, but not too soft or they will fall apart).

8. Remove from heat.

9. Add salt and garlic salt to taste.

Casseroles & Enchiladas

Rolled Red Chili Enchiladas

Ingredients:
2 dozen thin corn tortillas
1/2 pound grated Colby or
    Jack cheese
4 cups red chili sauce
1 cup canola oil
2 cups diced green onions
1 small can sliced black olives
    (optional)

1. Heat oil in frying pan until it bubbles.
2. Slightly fry tortillas (until soft).
3. Dip tortillas in red chili sauce.
4. Put green onions and cheese on tortillas and roll individually.
5. Pour remainder of chili sauce on top of rolled enchiladas.
6. Spread cheese over enchiladas.
7. Sprinkle green onions on top of enchiladas after sprinkling on the cheese.
8. Place sliced black olives over the enchiladas (optional).
9. Bake at 350 degrees until the cheese melts.

Red Chili Sauce: Boil 6 large chili pods (hot or mild with veins and stems removed) in water. When the chili pods turn bright red and are soft, remove from heat then remove pods from water. Let them cool and place them in blender on (low or puree) with 2 garlic cloves. Use water from pods as needed for thinner texture and salt to taste.

A Taste of Love from the Heart

 Note: For a quickie you can use Santa Cruz Chili
Paste and thin with water or broth.

Santa Cruz Chili and Spice Company process their own products
such as Santa Cruz Chili Red Chili Paste, Roasted Green Chili
Paste, dark 'Chile de Ristra' Chili Paste, Chipotle-Chile Paste and
Chipotle-Adobo Chili Paste. You will discover their unique blends
of flavor for authentic Southwest and Mexican cooking. These
products are excellent and easy for the customer to order. See
their website for additional information on their products.
www.santacruzchili.com/productss.html

A Taste of Love from the Heart

Rolled Green Chili Enchiladas

Ingredients:
2 dozen thin corn tortillas
4 cups shredded chicken (optional)
1/2 pound grated Colby or Jack cheese
2 cans cream of chicken soup
2 cans diced green chilies
1 cup canola oil

1. Heat oil until it begins to bubble.
2. Slightly fry tortillas until soft.
3. Dip tortillas in green sauce.
4. Place cheese and chicken on one side of tortilla and roll.
5. Pour remainder of chili sauce on each individual rolled enchilada.
6. Spread cheese over enchiladas.
7. Bake at 350 degrees until cheese melts.

Green Chili Sauce: Pour 2 cans cream of chicken soup into a medium saucepan; add 2 medium cans diced green chilies and stir mixture until texture is smooth. If mixture needs thinning, add milk; broth or water; your choice.

 Note: For extra hot flavor you can add diced jalapenos to taste.

Flat Red Enchiladas

Ingredients:
1/2 pound masa
1/2 cup cottage cheese
1/2 cup potato flakes
4 cups shredded chicken
   (optional)
2 cups diced steamed carrots
2 cups diced steamed
   potatoes
3 cups thinly shredded
   iceberg lettuce
1 cup diced steamed carrots
1 cup diced steamed
   potatoes
1/2 pound crumbled
   Mexican cheese (lightly
   salted)
4 cups red chili sauce
2 cups canola oil
1 cup diced green stuffed
   olives
1 cup diced white onion
1/4 cup white vinegar
1 teaspoon oregano
Salt/pepper to taste to taste

1. Place fresh corn masa in a medium size bowl (you can buy masa in grocery stores or at tortilla factory).

2. Add cottage cheese.

3. Add potato flakes.

4. Mix ingredient until texture is soft, but not sticky.

5. Make patties the size of a hamburger (1/4-inch thick) on waxed paper.

6. Heat oil in a frying pan and place patties evenly.

7. Fry on one side until golden brown and flip over; repeat.

8. Place patties in a loaf pan lined with a paper towel to drain off excess oil.

9. Mix vinegar, diced onion and oregano to marinate.

10. Use tongs to dip patties in red chili sauce.

11. Place shredded lettuce on top of dipped patty.

12. Place carrots, potatoes, onions and olives on top of lettuce and sprinkle with cheese.

A Taste of Love from the Heart

Red Chili Sauce: Boil 6 large chili pods (hot or mild with veins and stems removed) in water. When the chili pods turn bright red and are soft, remove from heat then remove pods from water. Let them cool and place them in blender on (low or puree) with 2 garlic cloves. Use water from pods as needed for thinner texture and salt to taste.

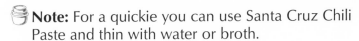**Note:** For a quickie you can use Santa Cruz Chili Paste and thin with water or broth.

Green Chili/Chicken Enchilada Casserole

Ingredients:
4 shredded chicken
   breast/seasoned
1/2 pound grated Jack
   cheese
2 cans cream of chicken soup
1 large can green chili
   enchilada sauce
1 large bag white corn tortilla
   chips
1 pint sour cream
Salt/pepper to taste

1. Spread 1 cup sauce on the bottom of a 9-inch rectangular glass dish.
2. Spread one layer of chips on top of sauce.
3. Spread half of the shredded chicken.
4. Spread half of the cheese.
5. Spread sauce on top.
6. Repeat layering process and top with cheese.
7. Bake in 350 degree pre-heated oven for 20 to 25 minutes.
8. Test with fork to make sure chips are soft.

Sauce: In a small saucepan mix chicken soup; green chili enchilada sauce and sour cream and place on low heat; stir until blended.

Hamburger Beef Enchilada Casserole

Ingredients:
2 dozen corn tortillas
1 pound lean hamburger meat
2 cans cream of mushroom
  soup
1 pint sour cream
2 cans diced green chilies
Salt/pepper/garlic salt to taste
2 cloves garlic, diced
1 cup diced yellow onion
3 cups canola oil
3 cups grated Jack cheese

1. Sauté onion and garlic in 1 tablespoon canola oil.
2. Add hamburger and fry until cooked.
3. Season to taste with salt; pepper and garlic salt.
4. Mix cream of mushroom soup; sour cream; diced green chilies; in a medium size bowl.
5. Soft fry tortillas in hot oil by turning on both sides.
6. Spread 1 cup mixture in a 9-inch rectangular glass dish.
7. Place 1 layer of tortillas on top of mixture.
8. Place half of hamburger meat on tortillas.
9. Pour half of remaining soup mixture on top of hamburger.
10. Spread half of the cheese.
11. Repeat layering process and top with cheese.
12. Bake in 350 degree pre-heated oven for 20 minutes.

Red Chili/Chicken Enchilada Casserole

Ingredients:
4 seasoned chicken breasts, shredded
1/2 pound grated Longhorn cheese
2 cans cream of mushroom soup
2 cans diced green chilies
1 large bag Fritos
1 can sliced black olives
2 cups red chili sauce

1. Spread 1 cup sauce on bottom of a 9-inch rectangular glass dish.
2. Spread one layer of chips on top of sauce.
3. Add a layer of half the chicken.
4. Add a layer of half the cheese.
5. Spread sauce on top.
6. Repeat layering process and top with cheese.
7. Bake in 350 degree pre-pre-heated oven for 20 to 25 minutes.
8. Test with fork to make sure chips are soft.

Red chili Sauce: Boil 6 large chili pods (hot or mild with veins and stems removed) in water. When the chili pods turn bright red and are soft, remove from heat then remove pods from water. Let them cool and place them in blender on (low or puree) with 2 garlic cloves. Use water from pods as needed for thinner texture and salt to taste.

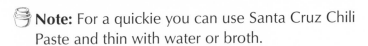 **Note:** For a quickie you can use Santa Cruz Chili Paste and thin with water or broth.

Chili Relleno Casserole

Ingredients:
12 fresh peeled and roasted green chilies with stem or 1 large can whole green chilies
2 cups milk
3 eggs
1/2 cup flour
1 pound grated Longhorn cheese
1 teaspoons salt

1. Place chilies on a greased 9-inch x 15-inch glass dish, with stems hanging over dish on both sides.

2. Layer cheese over chilies and repeat layering process.

3. Mix milk; eggs; flour and salt.

4. Pour mixture over layers and cover with remaining cheese.

5. Bake in pre-heated 350 degree oven for 45 minutes or crispy on top (do not cover).

Golden Mushroom Macaroni Casserole

Ingredients:
1 pound lean hamburger meat
2 small cans golden mushroom soup
1 large 8 oz. package of cream cheese
1/2 cup grated Longhorn or Colby cheese
Salt/pepper/garlic salt to taste

1. Sauté hamburger in medium skillet.
2. In a medium pot melt cream cheese.
3. Boil macaroni until semi-soft and drain in cold water.
4. Add golden mushroom soup to cream cheese and stir until well blended.
5. Add macaroni and stir.
6. Add hamburger and stir
7. Pour mixture into a glass dish.
8. Sprinkle cheese on top.
9. Bake at 400 degrees in pre- heated oven for 10 minutes or until cheese has melted.

In honor of my Aunt Mary (Tuchi) who has passed on, I thank her for sharing this macaroni casserole recipe with me. I remember her inviting us over for dinner at her little apartment and my son Jody was counting the minutes until we ate (as his Tata would say "feed this child, he's twisted"), but he loved this side dish she prepared. I have since shared it with many of my friends (a great kid's dish). Not only is it simple, but it went a long ways. I thank you Aunt Tuchi and may you rest in peace with the Lord.

Broccoli Casserole

Ingredients:

1 cup Minute Rice
1/4 cup water
4 tablespoons of margarine
1 small can cream of chicken
    soup
1/2 cup of milk
1 small jar of Cheese Whiz
2 small boxes of frozen
    chopped broccoli
1 cup diced brown onion
Salt to taste

1. In a small skillet sauté diced onion with margarine.

2. In a medium bowl combine cream of chicken soup, milk, water and stir.

3. Add the sauté diced onions.

4. Add uncooked rice.

5. Add drained broccoli.

6. Add Cheese Whiz.

7. Stir all ingredients together and place in a medium glass dish.

8. Bake in pre-heated 350 degree oven for 1 hour.

Hamburger and Green Chili Casserole

Ingredients:
1 pound lean hamburger
   meat
1 small can cream of
   mushroom soup
2 cup of milk
2 cups sour cream
2 small cans green chili
1 pound egg noodles
Salt/pepper/garlic salt to taste

1. Sauté hamburger in medium skillet.
2. Add salt/peper/garlic salt to taste.
3. Add green chiles.
4. In a medium pot combine cream of mushroom soup with milk and stir.
5. Combine hamburger mixture with cream of mushroom mixture and stir.
6. Cook mixture on medium low heat for 10 minutes.
7. Boil egg noodle until semi-soft and drain in cold water.
8. Pour hamburger mixture over noodles and serve.

Chicken & Pork Dishes

A Taste of Love from the Heart

Cacciatore Chicken

Ingredients:

1 large package skinless chicken pieces with bone

1 small yellow onion; sliced in strips

1 small green bell pepper, sliced in strips

1 can of stewed tomatoes

1 medium can sliced mushrooms

1 small can tomato sauce

1 teaspoon diced garlic

1 tablespoon basil (dried or fresh)

1 tablespoon oregano

1/3 cup olive oil

1/2 cup water

1 tablespoon crumbled/crushed bay leaf (dried or fresh)

Salt/pepper/onion salt/garlic salt to taste

1. In a large electric skillet heat oil and add seasoned chicken and garlic.

2. Let chicken brown.

3. Add onion, bell pepper mushrooms and stir for 1 minute.

4. Add stewed tomatoes.

5. Add tomato sauce.

6. Add water.

7. Add basil, oregano and bay leaf.

8. Add salt; pepper; onion salt and garlic salt to taste.

9. Simmer at 250 to 300 degrees for 1 hour in covered skillet.

10. Cut chicken to test if it is cooked thoroughly.

11. Serve over spaghetti, linguine or white rice.

Tip: Drop noodles in boiling salt water and add 1 drop of oil; boil for 1 minute and lower heat to medium; cook noodles until semi-soft (should be a little hard); rinse and drain in colander and always with cold water.

Cornish Hens with Plum Sauce

Ingredients:
2 Cornish hens split in half
1/2 stick of melted margarine
1 small bottle of honey

1. Place chicken pieces in a medium covered glass dish.
2. Rub margarine on hens with a pastry brush.
3. Season hens with salt; onion salt; garlic salt and lemon pepper to taste.
4. Drizzle honey over the hens.
5. Bake in pre-heated 325 degree oven for 1 hour.
6. Serve with plum sauce over hens.

Plum Sauce: Place 1 can whole plums with juice in a small pot and let it cook slow over medium heat for approximately 1 hour; mix 1 1/2 teaspoons of cornstarch with 1/4 cup water and make a paste; stir paste into the plum mixture and add 1 teaspoon sugar or Splenda and stir until sauce is semi-thin.

Cornflake Chicken Bake

Ingredients:

2 pounds skinned chicken pieces of your choice

2 teaspoons yellow mustard sauce

4 teaspoons vinegar

2 teaspoons salt

1 teaspoon paprika

1 teaspoon Worchester sauce

1 teaspoon Tabasco sauce

1 cup milk

1 1/2 cups of corn flake crumbs

1. In a medium bowl; combine mustard; vinegar; salt; paprika; Worchester sauce; Tabasco sauce; milk mustard sauce and stir.

2. Dip chicken pieces in sauce mixture.

3. Roll chicken pieces in corn flake crumbs.

4. Bake in pre-heated oven at 350 degrees for 1 hour.

Cranberry Chicken Dump

Ingredients:

2 pounds skinned chicken
   pieces of your choice
1 small bottle French dressing
1 medium can of whole
   cranberry sauce
1 package Lipton onion soup
1 small can whole or sliced
   black olives

1. Place chicken in a large rectangular glass dish.
2. Mix dressing; cranberry sauce; onion soup in a medium size mixing bowl and stir.
3. Pour mixture over raw unsalted chicken.
4. Sprinkle olives over chicken.
5. Bake in a 350 degree pre-heated oven for 1 hour.

Green Chili/Cheese Chicken Rolls

Ingredients:
6 skinned boneless chicken
   breasts
1/2 pound Jack cheese
2 sticks of real butter
1 teaspoon salt
1 teaspoon pepper
1 teaspoon garlic salt
1 teaspoon onion salt
1 teaspoon paprika
Round pointed toothpicks

1. Season both sides of chicken with salt; pepper; garlic salt and onion salt.

2. Place fresh green chili or whole canned chili on top of chicken breasts.

3. Cut strips of cheese and place on top of chili.

4. Roll chicken tucking in the ends and use a toothpick to hold together.

5. In a large skillet, melt 2 sticks of butter;- place chicken rolls in butter and sprinkle with paprika.

6. Place lid on the skillet and cook on medium low for 20 to 25 minutes.

Tip: A Teflon non-stick wok or large skillet works well for this dish. You can pound the chicken down with a meat tenderizer if it is too thick and it will make it easier to roll.

Pipian Chicken

Ingredients:
2 cups red chili sauce
3 tablespoons creamy peanut butter
1/2 cup evaporated milk
8 to 10 chicken thighs (or your favorite chicken parts)
Salt/pepper/onion salt/garlic salt to taste

1. Boil chicken parts in water until tender (but not falling apart).
2. Remove from broth and cool.
3. In a deep skillet melt the creamy peanut butter.
4. Add red chili sauce.
5. Add milk and stir.
6. Sprinkle salt, pepper, onion salt and garlic salt to taste.
7. Add chicken parts to sauce and let simmer on low for 20 minutes; covered.

Red Chili Sauce: Boil 6 large chili pods (hot or mild with veins and stems removed) in water. When the chili pods turn bright red and are soft, remove from heat then remove pods from water. Let them cool and place them in blender on (low or puree) with 2 garlic cloves. Use water from pods as needed for thinner texture and salt to taste.

Note: For a quickie you can use Santa Cruz Chili Paste and thin with water or broth.

Many of the older generation folks used roasted pumpkin seeds, but you can substitute creamy peanut butter for this dish. Be easy on the peanut butter, that is the secret; too much can over power the wonderful savors of the red chili. This dish is great with green corn tamales and beans!

Rocky Point Grilled Chicken

Ingredients:
2 pounds skinned chicken
    pieces
Fresh lime juice
Fresh crushed garlic
1/2 beer of your choice
1 cup soy sauce
2 tablespoons mustard sauce
Garlic salt

1. Rub fresh crushed garlic on chicken pieces (crushed garlic paste in a jar works well) and lime juice; sprinkle with garlic salt.

2. In a large covered mixing bowl combine soy sauce; beer; pepper and mustard sauce and stir.

3. Add chicken pieces to mixture; cover and refrigerate for 1 to 2 hours.

4. Grill until cooked.

Tomatillo Chicken

Ingredients:
2 pounds skinned chicken
   pieces
10 small green tomatillos
1 small bunch cilantro
1 or 2 Serrano chilies
3 fresh garlic cloves
3 diced green onions
Salt/pepper to taste

1. Remove leaves and skin of tomatillos and boil until tender.

2. In blender add cilantro; Serrano chili; green onion; garlic clove; sprinkle with salt and pepper; mix until pureed.

3. Bake or grill chicken.

4. Pour mixture over cooked chicken.

5. Bake at 350 degrees in pre-heated oven for 10 minutes.

Grilled Pork Chops with Chipotle Sauce

Ingredients:
4 Bone-in center cut 1/2- inch thick pork chops
Salt/pepper to taste
Onion salt/garlic salt to taste
1 cup raspberry chipotle or mango chipotle sauce

1. Wash chops and season with salt, pepper, onion salt and garlic salt on both sides.

2. Baste chops with either raspberry chipotle or mango chipotle sauce.

3. Grill (barbeque) on one side on medium heat for 6 minutes then flip (slit with knife to make sure it is well cooked).

4. Serve apples with chops (see recipe below).

Pecan Apples: Place 4 to 5 sliced and peeled red delicious apples in a skillet; add 1/2 cup Splenda; add 1/2 cup chopped sliced pecans; 1 tablespoon cinnamon; 1/2 cup rum; 1/2 brandy and stir until mixture begins to thicken and apples are soft.

Tip: You can alternate the apples for the following fruit: apricots; pears; plums and peaches. Follow the same instructions as above.

Pecan Ham

Ingredients:
1 bone-in fully cooked ham
1 1/2 cups chopped pecans
1 can of 7-Up
1 1/3 cups melted margarine
1 cup brown sugar
2 tablespoons mustard
1 can of sliced pineapples
1 small jar red maraschino
    cherries

1. In a glass dish, place flat end of ham face down.
2. Rub mustard on ham with a pastry brush.
3. Pour 7-Up over ham.
4. Bake in pre-heated oven at 400 degrees for 30 minutes and let cool.
5. In a pie tin, pound and crush pecans until well pulverized (almost powdery).
6. Combine nuts and margarine with brown sugar.
7. Pat down mixture over the rind of the ham.
8. Arrange pineapple slices on the flat side of the ham and insert cherries in the center holes of the pineapple.
9. Place ham back in the oven on its side for 15 minutes.

Rind side of ham

Flat side of ham

A Taste of Love from the Heart

Notes

Meat Dishes

(Beef)

Barbacoa

(shredded meat)

Ingredients:
1 large boneless cross-rib
 roast
1/4 cup diced garlic
1 tablespoon oregano
1 cup Worchester sauce
1 capful liquid smoke
Salt/pepper to taste
Onion salt/garlic salt to taste

1. Place meat in a covered dish or cast iron covered pot.

2. Add garlic; oregano; Worchester sauce; liquid smoke; heavily sprinkle with salt; pepper; onion salt and garlic salt.

3. Cook in a 225 degree pre-heated oven for 8 hours (overnight for best results) or until meat falls apart with knife and fork.

Berrilla

(shredded meat with red chili)

Ingredients:

1 large boneless cross-rib roast
1/4 cup diced garlic
1 cup diced white onion
1/4 cup white vinegar
1 can diced green chilies
3 cups V-8 vegetable juice
2 small diced tomatoes
1 cup chili paste
1 tablespoon oregano
Salt/pepper to taste
Onion salt/garlic salt to taste
1 dozen small corn tortillas

1. Place roast in a slow cooker and add 2 cups of water.
2. Cook for approximately 8 hours on low or until meat falls apart.
3. Use a knife and fork to shred meat.
4. Add fresh garlic.
5. Add vinegar.
6. Add 1/2 cup diced white onion.
7. Add green chili; V-8 vegetable juice; remainder of white onion; chili paste and fresh tomatoes.
8. Season to taste with salt; pepper; garlic salt and onion salt.
9. Let simmer on low for 1 hour.
10. Serve on small corn tortillas (shredded cabbage optional).

Beef Braising Ribs

Ingredients:
2 packages braising ribs
Salt/pepper to taste
Onion salt/garlic salt to taste
2 tablespoons powdered
    oregano

1. Place ribs flat in a glass rectangular dish.

2. Sprinkle salt; pepper; onion salt; garlic salt and powdered oregano; heavily on both sides of ribs.

3. Place in 350 degree pre-heated oven for 2 hours or until real tender.

When I think of these dishes, I think of my eldest son Jody at the age of eleven preparing the ribs for dinner and following the instructions over the phone. And now the trend continues and he volunteers dishes like Carne Con Chili for work and will still call and follow instructions over the phone and as usual it came out great! Both sons turned out to be excellent cooks.

Carne Con Chili

Ingredients:
2 pounds beef stew meat
1/4 cup chopped garlic
1 cup red chili sauce
1/4 cup flour
1/4 cup canola oil
1/2 cup water
Salt/pepper/onion salt/garlic
    salt to taste

1. Cut stew meat in small cubed pieces.
2. Roll meat in flour and sauté with garlic in canola oil on low heat for (10 minutes).
3. Add red chili sauce.
4. Season with salt; pepper; onion salt and garlic salt to taste.
5. Stir in water to thin if meat mixture is too thick.
6. Cover and simmer on medium low for 20 minutes or until meat is tender.

Red Chili Sauce: Boil 6 large chili pods (hot or mild and remove veins and stems) in water; when the chili pods turn bright red and are soft; remove from heat then remove pods from water and let them cool and place them in blender on (low or puree) with 2 garlic cloves; use water from pods as needed for thinner texture and salt to taste

Note: For a quickie you can use Santa Cruz Chili Paste and thin with water or broth

Carne Machaca

(Jerky)

Ingredients:
2 thin flank steaks
1/2 cup green onions
1/2 cup diced tomatoes
1/2 cup diced bell pepper
1 tablespoon garlic
1/2 cup chopped cilantro
Salt/pepper to taste
Onion salt/garlic salt to taste

1. Sprinkle salt; pepper; onion salt; garlic salt heavily on both sides of steaks.

2. Place seasoned steaks half way over a clean string and hang to dry in an indoor porch area.

3. Cover meat with netting so flies can not contact.

4. Dry for about a week or two; or until thoroughly dry.

5. Pound meat with stone bowl and rock (molcajete and tejote, see picture on page 108) until string like effect.

6. Place in meat in skillet with oil and stir.

7. Add garlic and vegetables.

8. Salt/pepper to taste.

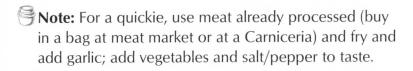**Note:** For a quickie, use meat already processed (buy in a bag at meat market or at a Carniceria) and fry and add garlic; add vegetables and salt/pepper to taste.

London Broil

Ingredients:
1 thick London broil steak
(approximately 3 pounds)
1 cup soy sauce
1 cup Worchester sauce
2 tablespoons peppercorns

1. In a bowl mix soy sauce, Worchester sauce and peppercorns (reserve 1 cup marinade).
2. Place meat in a covered bowl with marinade and refrigerate for 6 hours or overnight.
3. Grill on medium heat for 7 minutes on one side then 7 minutes on other side (do not turn);10 minutes on each side for well done.
4. Slice with an electric knife and place on serving dish.
5. Pour reserved cup of marinade on top of meat.
6. Place in microwave for 10 seconds and serve with sauté mushrooms.

Sautéed Mushrooms

Ingredients:
2 pounds fresh mushrooms
3 cloves fresh garlic
1/2 cup white wine
Salt/garlic salt to taste

1. Clean and slice mushrooms (use scrub brush; do not use water as they already contain water).
2. In a large skillet sauté garlic and butter.
3. Add wine.
4. Add garlic and salt to taste.

A Taste of Love from the Heart

Meat Loaf

Ingredients:
2 pounds lean hamburger
  meat
1 1/2 cups bread crumbs
2 eggs
1 package Lipton Onion
  Soup
3/4 cups water
1/3 cup catsup
1 small can sliced mushrooms
1/4 teaspoons salt
1/4 teaspoons pepper

1. In a medium bowl combine meat; bread crumbs; eggs; Lipton Onion Soup; catsup and water.

2. Add salt and pepper and mix well.

3. Spread mixture on waxed paper (12 inches long).

4. Spread sliced mushrooms on mixture.

5. Roll meat into a jelly roll and tuck ends.

6. Place on a glass dish and bake in pre-heated 350 degree oven for 35 minutes or until golden brown. In microwave 11 minutes turn dish and another 11 minutes.

Skirt Steak—Grilled

Ingredients:
1 package of skirt steak
1/3 cup crushed
2 tablespoon crushed
    oregano leaves
1 small can of beer
Salt/pepper/onion salt/garlic
    salt to taste

1. Pound meat down with tenderizing tool.
2. Place meat down in a covered container.
3. Place oregano in hands and rub hands back and forth over the meat till thoroughly crushed.
4. Heavily season the meat with salt, pepper, onion salt and garlic salt.
5. Pour 1 can of beer over the meat and place in the refrigerator for 2 days.
6. Remove meat from beer marinate.
7. Place on high heated grill for approximately 10 minutes flipping back and forth on both sides
8. Great with fresh chile verde and flour tortillas (see fresh chile verde recipe on page 110 and flour tortilla recipe on page 165).

A Taste of Love from the Heart

Swedish Cabbage Rolls

Ingredients:
1 head green cabbage leaves
1 pound lean ground beef
1 cup Minute Rice
1 egg
1/2 cup diced white onion
1/4 cup diced green bell
    pepper
1 small can tomato sauce
1 teaspoon salt
1 teaspoon pepper
1 stick melted butter
1 cup Longhorn grated
    cheese

1. In a medium bowl combine meat; egg; onion and bell pepper.

2. Add rice and 1/2 can of tomato sauce.

3. Add salt and pepper and mix well.

4. Boil lettuce leaves until semi soft.

5. Remove leaves from water and place on a paper towel to drain.

6. Place 1/2 stick of melted butter in a square glass dish.

7. Place mixture on top center of leaf (approximately 2 tablespoons); tuck sides and roll; hold with a toothpick.

8. Pour remainder of melted butter on top of rolls.

9. Bake in 325 degree pre-heated oven for 1 hour (add tomato sauce and cheese last 10 minutes).

Tripas De Leche

(Tripe Milk Glands)

Ingredients:

2 packages of tripas
2 tablespoons powdered
  oregano
Salt, pepper, onion salt and
  garlic salt to taste

1. Clean an unravel tripas.
2. Place in a glass dish and season with oregano; salt; pepper; onion salt and garlic salt.
3. Bake in 400 degree pre-heated oven for 15 minutes.
4. Use a sharp knife and puncture each puffed gland to remove excess milk and continue baking at 350 degrees for about 1 hour.
5. Remove tripas from grease and place in a clean dish and bake until tripas are crispy like bacon (do not dry out and overcook).
6. Cut tripas in small 3-inch pieces.

Tip: Great with flour tortillas and fresh green chili salsa (See pages 110 and 165 for tortilla recipes and green chili salsa recipe)

Notes

Pasta & Sauce

Lasagna

Ingredients:
1 package cooked noodles
1/4 cup melted butter
1 drop olive oil

Meatballs:
2 pounds lean hamburger meat
1 1/2 cups bread crumbs
5 eggs
1 slice white bread soaked in water
3 tablespoons grated Parmesan cheese
1/4 teaspoon salt
1/4 teaspoon pepper
1/4 teaspoon garlic powder
1/4 cup bacon grease
2 chopped garlic cloves

Filling:
2 containers Ricotta cheese
1 pound grated Mozzarella cheese
1 cup grated Parmesan cheese

1. Combine in medium bowl meatball ingredients: meat; bread crumbs; eggs; soaked bread; Parmesan cheese and garlic powder.
2. Roll into small meat balls.
3. Brown meat balls in garlic cloves and bacon grease.
4. Boil noodles in salt water with 1 drop of oil for 1 minute. Lower heat to medium and cook noodles until semi-soft.
5. Rinse and drain in colander with cold water.
6. Pour melted butter evenly in a rectangular glass dish.
7. Layer noodles across dish.
8. Divide meat into 3 parts.
9. Mash 1 part of meatballs on noodles (repeat for each of 3 layers).
10. Add sauce; Parmesan; dotted Ricotta and Mozzarella (repeat for each of 3 layers).
11. Bake in pre-heated 350 degree oven for 45 minutes to 1 hour.

Tip: Always rinse pasta in cold water and leave a little hard (semi-soft); do not overcook.

Red Sauce

(Use same recipe for lasagna and spaghetti)

Ingredients:

1 large can peeled whole tomatoes (mash by squeezing with your hands)

2 small cans tomato paste

2 large can tomato puree

1 can of water for each can of tomato paste; puree; tomatoes; 4 total cans

2 tablespoons basil

2 tablespoons oregano

2 tablespoons parsley

1 teaspoon crushed bay leaf

1/4 teaspoon each: salt/pepper/ garlic powder/onion powder

1/4 cup sherry wine

1 teaspoon crushed red pepper (optional)

1. In a large covered pot add whole mashed tomatoes; tomato paste; tomato puree and stir.

2. Add basil; oregano; parsley and crushed bay leaf.

3. Add salt; pepper; garlic powder and onion powder.

4. Add sherry wine.

5. Cook on low for 2 to 3 hours (the longer the better).

6. Mushrooms and red peppers are optional.

7. For spaghetti with meat sauce add crushed meatballs to sauce.

Pesto Sauce

Ingredients:
1/4 cup butter
1/4 cup olive oil
1/4 cup grated Parmesan
cheese
1 garlic clove
Dash of salt
1/4 cup chopped pine nuts
1/2 cup fresh basil leaves

1. Combine in blender: butter; oil; cheese; garlic; basil leaves and salt.

2. Add finely chopped pine nuts and whirl quickly in blender until smooth yet coarse consistency.

3. Refrigerate for 20 minutes.

4. Serve over spaghetti or fettuccine.

Notes

Rice & Calabasitas

Spanish Rice

Ingredients:
2 cups Minute Rice
1/2 cup canola oil
1 tablespoon garlic
1/4 cup diced brown onion
1/4 cup celery
1/4 cup fresh cilantro
1 small can tomato sauce
1 cup frozen mixed peas and
    carrots
1 1/2 cups chicken broth
Salt/pepper to taste

1. Place oil in a skillet and heat.
2. When hot add rice, garlic and brown.
3. Add onion and celery.
4. Add broth and cover for 5 minutes or until firm.
5. Stir and add cilantro.
6. Place in rectangular microwave dish; add mixed peas and carrots on top.
7. Place in microwave for 3 to 4 minutes (cover with paper towel to remove some of the excess moisture).

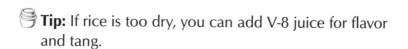 **Tip:** If rice is too dry, you can add V-8 juice for flavor and tang.

Fried Rice

Ingredients:
1 1/2 cups long grain rice
1/2 cube margarine
1 small diced Roma tomato
1/2 cup diced bell pepper
1 package Lipton Onion Soup
Water
Salt/pepper to taste

1. In a medium sauce pan melt margarine.
2. Add long grain rice.
3. Add tomato and bell pepper.
4. Mix in Lipton Onion Soup.
5. Add water to cover 1/2-inch above ingredients.
6. Boil for 5 minutes.
7. Cover and let simmer until rice mixture is soften but yet a little crunchy.

Tia Techi, thank you for sharing the fried rice recipe with me. I was able to invent other rice dishes by mistakenly leaving out ingredients and I decided to alter the recipe and that is how the white mushroom rice was invented. You were always a great cook!

White Mushroom Rice

Ingredients:
2 cups Minute rice
1 cup margarine
1/2 cup diced celery
1/4 cup diced green bell
1/4 cup diced red bell
  pepper
1/4 cup diced white onion
1 small can sliced mushrooms
Salt/pepper/garlic salt/onion
  salt to taste

1. In a medium sauce pan melt margarine.
2. Add Minute rice
3. Add vegetables.
4. Add can of drained mushrooms.
5. Add 3/4 cup water.
6. Boil for 5 minutes.
7. Cover and let simmer till rice mixture is soften, but still a little firm.
8. Season with salt/pepper/ onion salt/garlic salt to taste.

Calabasitas

(Zucchini)

Ingredients:
4 large zucchini diced in medium cubes
3/4 cup diced brown onion
1 can yellow corn
2 diced small tomatoes
1 lb chunked Quesadilla cheese or grated Jack cheese
Salt/pepper/garlic salt/onion salt to taste

1. In a medium size pot boil zucchini and onions till semi-soft.
2. Drain out water.
3. Add tomatoes.
4. Add can of corn.
5. Add cheese.
6. Season with salt, pepper, onion salt and garlic salt to taste.
7. Stir all ingredients.
8. Cover and let simmer on low for 25 minutes.

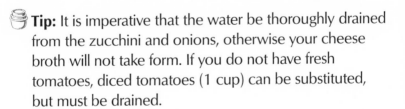 **Tip:** It is imperative that the water be thoroughly drained from the zucchini and onions, otherwise your cheese broth will not take form. If you do not have fresh tomatoes, diced tomatoes (1 cup) can be substituted, but must be drained.

Calabasitas are one of my family's favorite side dishes. The savory white sauce that is attained by the cheese and other flavors is such a delight to devour. I will usually make a large quantity so that doggy bags can be carted home for lunches. It goes great with almost any Mexican dish.

Notes

_____

_____

_____

_____

_____

_____

_____

_____

_____

_____

_____

_____

_____

_____

_____

_____

_____

_____

_____

_____

_____

Salads

Angel Hair Marinated Salad

Ingredients

1 pound cooked angel hair pasta
1 cup diced raw carrots
1 cup diced celery
1 cup diced Roma tomatoes
1 cup diced green bell pepper
1 cup diced purple onion
1 cup Italian dressing
1/2 cup olive oil
Salt/pepper to taste

1. In a medium pot of boiling water add 1 drop of olive oil; add angel hair pasta; cook on medium heat until semi-hard.

2. Drain in colander and rinse with cold water.

3. Place pasta in an airtight covered container.

4. Add carrots; celery; tomatoes; bell pepper; and purple onion.

5. Stir in Italian dressing.

6. Refrigerate for 1 to 2 hours.

7. Salt/pepper to taste.

This is a light and cool side dish or salad. For variations in all of the salads you can also add cooked tiny shrimp, grilled steak or shredded chicken. Don't be afraid to be creative, you are in charge. I have made this dish in large scale for summer parties. Also, my Jimmy, wanted a party to celebrate his twenty-first birthday and his leaving home to take residence in Sierra Vista, where he would assume employment. I made this salad and it was a big hit with both family and his friends. It went great with the menu he ordered that consisted of smoked turkey, garlic shrimp, and London Broil (a party to remember).

A Taste of Love from the Heart

Green Cabbage Salad

Ingredients:

3 cups green cabbage (chunked into 2-inch pieces)

Romaine lettuce (2 leaves cut into 2-inch pieces)

3 cups Iceberg lettuce (chunked into 2-inch pieces)

1/2 peeled pomegranate fruit

1/2 cup coconut

1/2 cup green onion

1/2 cup thin sliced celery rings

1/2 cup chopped walnuts or pecans

1 small can mandarin oranges (drained)

Salt/pepper to taste

1. Chop lettuce and place into a medium size bowl.
2. Add cabbage.
3. Add drained oranges.
4. Add pomegranate fruit.
5. Add celery and green onions.
6. Add nuts.
7. Add coconut.
8. Salt/ pepper to taste.

Green Cranberry Salad

Ingredients:

2 cups fresh spinach (remove
  stems)
Romaine lettuce (4 leaves cut
  into 2-inch pieces)
Curly leaf lettuce (4 leaves
  cut into 2-inch pieces)
1 small can sliced black olives
1/4 cup jicama, grated
1/4 dried cranberries
1/4 golden raisins
1/4 grated carrots
1/4 walnuts; chopped
Salt/pepper to taste

1. Chop lettuce and place
   into a medium size bowl.
2. Add spinach.
3. Add drained olives.
4. Add raisins; cranberries;
   carrots and jicama.
5. Add walnuts.
6. Salt/pepper to taste.
7. Add salad dressing of your
   choice.

Green Cucumber Salad

Ingredients:
Romaine lettuce (4 leaves cut into 2-inch pieces)
3 cups Iceberg lettuce (chunked into 2-inch pieces)
1 cup peeled diced cucumber
1 avocado sliced
1 cup diced Roma tomatoes
1/2 cup green onion
1/2 cup cilantro
1/2 cup garbanzo beans
1/2 cup thin sliced celery rings
1/2 cup sliced almonds
Salt/pepper to taste

1. Chop lettuce and place into a medium size bowl.
2. Add cucumber and tomatoes.
3. Add avocados.
4. Add garbanzo beans.
5. Add celery; cilantro and green onions.
6. Add nuts.
7. Salt and pepper to taste.
8. Add salad dressing of your choice.

Green Pine Nut Salad

Ingredients:

2 cups fresh spinach with stems removed

4 leaves Romaine lettuce cut into 2-inch pieces

1 cup shredded purple cabbage

1/4 raw pine nuts

1/4 bacon bits

1/4 diced Roma tomatoes

1/4 diced celery

1/4 cup chopped cilantro

1/4 cup green onion

Salt/pepper to taste

1. Chop lettuce and place into a medium size bowl.
2. Add spinach.
3. Add purple cabbage.
4. Add bacon bits; celery; tomatoes; cilantro and green onions.
5. Add pine nuts.
6. Salt and pepper to taste.
7. Add salad dressing of your choice.

Macaroni Salad

Ingredients:
2 pounds salad macaroni
  (works best)
2 cups Best Food Mayonnaise
5 diced boiled eggs
1/2 cup diced celery
1/2 cups diced dill pickles
1/2 cup diced green onions
1/4 cup lemon juice
1/8 cup pickle juice
8 cups water
1 teaspoon olive oil or canola
1 large can sliced black olives
Salt/pepper/paprika to taste
Paprika for garnish

1. Boil water in a medium pot; add oil to water.

2. Add macaroni and lower heat to medium; remove when pasta is semi-soft but still firm.

3. Rinse pasta in cold water.

4. In large bowl combine: pasta; celery; pickles; onions; eggs and olives.

5. Stir in mayonnaise; lemon juice and pickle juice.

6. Season with salt/pepper and paprika to taste.

8. Sprinkle paprika lightly on top of salad for garnish.

Potato Salad

Ingredients:
5 large boiled Russet
  potatoes
2 cups mayonnaise
6 diced boiled eggs
1/2 cup diced celery
1/2 cup diced brown onions
8 cups water
1 large can sliced black olives
Salt/pepper to taste
Paprika for garnish

1. Boil water in a medium pot; add potatoes to water; lower heat to medium and cook until soft (approximately 1 hour).

2. Cool potatoes for 2 hours in fridge.

3. Boil eggs; peel; cool and dice.

4. In large bowl combine: cubed potatoes; celery; onions; eggs and olives.

5. Stir in mayonnaise.

6. Season with salt/pepper to taste.

7. Sprinkle paprika lightly on top of salad for garnish.

Potatoes Escabeche

(Marinated)

Ingredients:
5 large boiled Russet
  potatoes
1 cup thin stripped jalapenos
1 medium yellow onion cut in
  thin half slices
1 can of sliced carrots
1 cup vinegar
1 cup canola oil
1 tablespoon oregano
8 cups water
Salt/pepper to taste
2 cans tiny shrimp (optional)

1. Boil water in medium pot; add potatoes; lower heat to medium and cook until soft (approximately 1 hour).

2. Cool potatoes for 2 hours in fridge.

3. Marinate in a small bowl: onion slices; vinegar; oil and oregano for 1 hour and carrots in jalapeno juice.

4. Peel and slice potatoes approximately 1/3-inch thick.

5. In an airtight container layer: potatoes; onion; jalapeno strips; carrots and shrimp (optional).

6. Repeat layering process.

7. Pour onion marinate over layers and 1/2 cup jalapeno juice.

8. Season with salt/ pepper to taste.

9. Mix well and refrigerate overnight in the airtight container.

Salpicon Salad

(Combination of Vegetables/Beef or Tongue)

Ingredients:

1 large tongue or beef roast
1 medium brown onion cut in
  thin half slices
5 carrot sticks; steamed
3 zucchini; steamed
3 large brown potatoes;
  steamed
1 small head shredded
  iceberg lettuce
2 large hard sliced tomatoes
1 can of sliced beets
  (optional)
6 boiled eggs; sliced
1 tablespoon oregano
1/2 cup vinegar
1/2 cup salad oil
1/2 cup Best Food
  Mayonnaise
Salt/pepper to taste

1. Boil beef or tongue in a medium pot until soft but can slice (approximately 2 hours) on medium heat; cover and slice semi-thin when cool.

2. Steam potatoes; zucchini and carrots; cool for 20 minutes in fridge and slice.

3. Slice onions; tomatoes; eggs and lettuce.

4. Marinate in a small bowl: onion slices; vinegar; oil and oregano for 1 hour.

5. On platter layer potatoes; onions; meat; lettuce; tomatoes; eggs; carrots; zucchini; beets; season each layer with salt/pepper and place mayonnaise on top of lettuce and tomatoes.

6. If desired, spread excess marinate on top of vegetables.

Topopo Salad

Ingredients:

3 boiled and shredded chicken breasts

1 cup thin stripped jalapenos

1 small package frozen mixed peas/carrots

1 small head iceberg lettuce; shredded

2 small hard tomatoes; sliced

1 cup large pimento green olives

2 large avocados sliced in strips

1 cup grated Longhorn cheese

1 small pint cottage cheese

3 cups mashed beans

1 dozen thin corn tortillas

1 cup canola oil

2 cups Italian or vinegar and oil dressing

Salt/pepper to taste

1. Boil skinned chicken breasts; cool and shred into thin strips.

2. Fry tortillas flat until crispy; drain on a paper towel.

3. Heat up smashed beans (see page 25 for Smashed bean recipe).

4. Shred lettuce.

5. Slice tomatoes.

6. Grate cheese.

7. Defrost mixed peas/carrots.

8. Drain green olives.

9. Slice thin strips of avocados.

A Taste of Love from the Heart

Preparing Topopo Salad

1. Place 1 fried corn tortilla on a plate.
2. Spread beans on fried.
3. Spread a layer of lettuce on beans.
4. Spread chicken on top of lettuce and avocado strips.
5. Sprinkle mixed peas/carrots on lettuce.
6. Repeat process: lettuce; chicken and mixed peas/carrots 3 times (will be a small mountain shape).
7. Place a tomato slice on top of mountain.
8. Place 1 scoop of cottage cheese on top of tomato and top with a green olive.
9. Place avocado and jalapenos tips vertically on the mountain.
10. Sprinkle grated cheese all over mountain and season with salt/pepper to taste.
11. Individuals can put their own dressing according to preference.

A Taste of Love from the Heart

Notes

Salad Dressings

Balsamic Dressing

Ingredients:
1 1/2 cups honey
1 cup red wine
1 cup red wine vinegar
1 cup balsamic vinegar
2 cups salad oil
5 cloves fresh garlic
3 teaspoons oregano
3 teaspoons sweet basil

1. In blender combine red wine; red wine vinegar; and balsamic vinegar on low speed.
2. Add honey.
3. Add salad oil.
4. Blend for 10 seconds.
5. Add garlic.
6. Add oregano
7. Add sweet basil
8. Blend for 10 seconds.

Orange Dressing

Ingredients:
1/3 cup salad oil
1/4 cup orange juice
    concentrate
3 tablespoons white vinegar
1 clove minced garlic
1 teaspoon parsley
1 packet artificial sweetener
1/4 teaspoon salt

1. In blender mix salad oil; orange juice and vinegar on low speed.
2. Add garlic and parsley.
3. Sweeten with artificial sweetener to taste if too sour.
4. Add salt.
5. Blend at high speed for 1 minute.

Pineapple Dressing

Ingredients:
1/2 cup canned pineapple
2 tablespoons honey
2 tablespoons salad oil
2 tablespoons lemon juice
1/4 teaspoon salt
1/2 teaspoon pepper

1. In blender combine pineapple; honey; oil and lemon juice on low speed.
2. Add salt/pepper.
3. Blend at high speed for 1 minute.

Raspberry Dressing

Ingredients:
4 tablespoons raspberry jam
3 tablespoons white wine vinegar
2 tablespoons honey
4 teaspoons salad oil
1 clove of garlic

1. In blender combine raspberry jam; vinegar; wine; honey and salad oil on low speed.
2. Add garlic.
3. Blend on high speed for 1 minute.

Red Spice Dressing

Ingredients:

4 eggs
1 small white onion
1 tablespoon sugar
1 tablespoon salt
1 clove fresh garlic
2 tablespoons paprika
1 tablespoon dry mustard
1/2 cup vinegar
2 cups salad oil

1. In blender combine eggs; onion; sugar; salt; garlic; paprika; mustard on low speed.

2. Add vinegar and press pulse button for 2 seconds.

3. Add salad oil and press pulse button for 2 seconds.

4. Blend at high speed for 1 to 2 minutes.

Notes

Salsas

Fresh Chile Verde

(Fresh Green Chili)

Ingredients:
3 pounds roasted green chili
1/2 cup canola oil
5 large roasted tomatoes
1/4 cup diced garlic
Salt/pepper to taste

1. In a large skillet sauté garlic in 2 tablespoons oil.
2. Add fresh roasted tomatoes and mash.
3. Add fresh stripped green chili.
4. Season with salt/pepper to taste.

Roasted Tomatoes and Green Chili: Grease 5 large tomatoes and roast in the oven at 400 degrees until soft and toasty; use 3 pounds green roasted chili (roast same as tomatoes) chili will puff up and toast. You can also use store bought chili already roasted; peel and cut in strips.

Pico de Gallo

Ingredients:
5 diced tomatoes
1 diced medium white onion
1 cup chopped cilantro
2 diced large fresh raw jalapeños
2 diced large yellow raw Serrano chilies
1 small lime (optional)
Salt/pepper/onion salt/garlic salt to taste

1. Place onion in a medium bowl.
2. Add diced tomatoes.
3. Add chopped.
4. Add jalapeños.
5. Add Serrano chilies.
6. Add squeezed lime juice (optional).
7. Mix till well blended.
8. Season with salt/pepper/onion salt/garlic salt to taste.
9. Refrigerate salsa in tight plastic sealed container.

A Taste of Love from the Heart

Red Chili Chunk Salsa

Ingredients:
3 small cans diced green chili

1 large of can whole
    tomatoes
1 cup chopped cilantro
3 chilitepines
1/4 cup diced garlic
1/2 cup diced white onion
Salt/pepper to taste

1. Put onion in blender; use chop button for a few seconds.

2. Pour in can whole tomatoes.

3. Add cilantro; use chop button for a few seconds.

4. Add garlic and chilitepines.

5. Add green chilies press pulse button on and off until thick and chunky; not saucy.

6. Season with salt/pepper to taste.

Red Thin Salsa

Ingredients:
1 large can whole tomatoes
1 small bunch of cilantro
2 large jalapeños
4 cloves fresh garlic
1 tablespoon oregano
1/2 medium chopped yellow
  onion
Salt/pepper/onion salt/garlic
  salt to taste

1. Put onion in a blender; use chop button for a few seconds.
2. Pour in can of whole tomatoes.
3. Add cilantro; use chop button for a few seconds.
4. Add garlic.
5. Add oregano.
6. Add jalapeños.
7. Blend on high for 1 minute.
8. Season with salt/pepper/ onion salt/garlic salt to taste.
9. Blend on high for 2 more minutes and refrigerate salsa in tight plastic sealed container until salsa thickens.

Notes

Seafood

Abalone Cocktail

Ingredients:
1 large can of V-8 vegetable
   juice
1 can diced abalone
1 can of Veg-All
1 large can mixed
   peas/carrots
1 large can cut green beans
2 diced large jalapenos
1 cup jalapeno juice
2 cans tiny baby shrimp
   (optional)
Salt/pepper to taste

1. In a large covered container pour 1 can V-8 vegetable juice.
2. Add diced abalone.
3. Add shrimp (optional).
4. Add vegetables.
5. Add jalapenos.
6. Add jalapeno juice to taste.
7. Season with salt/pepper to taste.

Ceviche Soya/ Shrimp Cocktail

Ingredients:
2 cups Soya beans
1 small bottle of Clamato Juice
5 diced tomatoes
2 peeled diced cucumber
1 diced red onion
1 cup chopped cilantro
1 diced large fresh jalapeños
1 large fresh yellow Serrano chilies (optional)
1 can of tiny baby shrimp (optional)
Salt/pepper to taste

1. Boil 2 cups Soya beans for 5 minutes and let stand for 15 minutes.
2. In a medium bowl add diced tomatoes.
3. Add diced cucumber.
4. Add cilantro.
5. Add red onion.
6. Add jalapeños/Serrano chilies.
7. Add Soya beans (will form like clams when cooked).
8. Add shrimp (optional).
9. Add Clamato juice and mix until well blended.
10. Season with salt/pepper to taste.

A Taste of Love from the Heart

Garlic Shrimp & Butter

Ingredients:
2 pounds cleaned shrimp
   with shell
3 cloves of whole garlic
1 stick of butter
1 lemon
1 cup orange juice
Salt/garlic salt to taste

1. In a skillet sauté butter and garlic.

2. Add shrimp.

3. Add squeezed lemon juice.

4. Add orange juice.

5. Season heavily with salt/garlic salt to taste.

6. Cover and simmer on low until shrimp turns pink and is tender (approximately 10 minutes); be sure not to overcook or shrimp will be rubbery.

Lobster Tails & Butter

Ingredients:
4 lobster tails
1 cup mayonnaise
1 cup melted butter
Paprika
Salt/pepper to taste

1. In a medium pot place lobster tails in boiling water until pink (approximately 10 minutes).

2. Remove immediately from water and place on a cookie sheet.

3. Spread 1/4-inch layer of mayonnaise on lobster meat (mayo is a tenderizer).

4. Sprinkle salt/pepper and paprika.

5. Place in broiler for 5 to 10 minutes (edges will get dark and crispy; do not over cook or will become rubbery).

6. Serve with melted butter and your favorite side dishes.

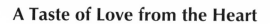

Notes

Soups

A Taste of Love from the Heart

Soup, one of my favorite meals, I could eat soup every day. During my childhood years we had soup quite often. Not only is it nourishing and filling, but it is also very soothing to the stomach.

I raised my sons on soup in very much the same manner as how I was nurtured. There were many occasions when money was short and times were tough, but soup was inexpensive to make and quite satisfying. Home made tortillas and soup always did the trick!

And now the tradition goes on. I have the pleasure of making soups and tortillas for my grandbabies and they too can experience that special love that Nanie makes for them.

I let the grandchildren assist me in the kitchen and let them be a part of preparing the meal. This little pleasure makes them feel very special and it also gives them an incentive to pursue cooking when they mature. My oldest grandchild is already asking at the young age of three and a half years, if I will teach her how to make various dishes when she grows up, or will I let her place the tortillas on the grill when she is old enough. I explain to her the dangers involved with the hot grill and she accepts my explanation without any argument.

Children need that old fashion remedy called guidance. If you guide them down the right path in life they will experience a sense of satisfaction and gratification. It is no different with cooking; children can learn to be creative, decisive and content. I used some of the recipes and preparation of these dishes in some of my college presentations to demonstrate various factors such as time, organization development and preparation.

And now if you will follow me to the next page, I will take you on my journey to visit the Land of SOUP!

Abondigas

Meatball Soup

Ingredients:

1 cup Minute Rice
1 pound lean hamburger
   meat
1 egg
1/4 cup celery
1/4 green bell pepper
1/4 diced tomatoes
1/4 green onion
1/4 fresh cilantro
10 cups water
3 tablespoons; Knorr Caldo
   deTomate powder
1/2 small can tomato sauce
Salt/pepper/garlic salt/onion
   salt to taste

1. In a medium bowl combine meat; egg; rice; dash of salt/pepper.
2. Roll meat into small balls.
3. Boil water in a medium size covered pot.
4. Drop in meatballs; cook until firm.
5. Remove any scum from top.
6. Add Knorr Caldo de Tomate and stir.
7. Add tomato sauce.
8. Add vegetables.
9. Season with salt/pepper/ onion salt/garlic salt to taste.
10. Cover and simmer on low for 45 minutes.

Arroz Con Pollo

Chicken Rice Soup

Ingredients:

10 cups water
2 cans chicken broth
2 cups long grain rice
2 tablespoons canola oil
1 cup sliced carrots
1 pound semi-cooked chicken
    wings
1/4 small celery slices
1/4 cup of green onion
1/4 cup of fresh cilantro
3 tablespoons; Knorr Caldo
    deTomate powder
Salt/pepper/garlic salt/onion
    salt to taste

1. In a medium sized pot brown rice in oil.
2. Add water and chicken broth & Knorr Caldo de Tomate powder.
3. Add celery; cilantro; carrots and onions.
4. Add chicken wings.
5. Season with salt/pepper/ onion salt/garlic salt to taste.
6. Cook on medium heat for 1 hour or until vegetables are soft.

A Taste of Love from the Heart

Caldo De Macaron

Macaroni Soup

Ingredients:
1/2 pound elbow macaroni
2 large zucchini; diced in very small cubes
1 package stew meat; diced in very small cubes
1 cup thinly sliced celery
2 tablespoons canola oil
2 cans chicken broth
5 cups water
Salt/pepper/celery salt/garlic salt/onion salt to taste

1. In a medium size pot brown macaroni in oil.
2. Add broth and water.
3. Add cubed meat.
4. Add zucchini and celery.
5. Cover and turn heat to medium for 1 hour.
6. Season with salt/pepper/celery salt/garlic salt/onion salt to taste.

Caldo De Queso

Cheese Soup

Ingredients:
4 large Russet potatoes, peeled
and diced in medium cubes
2 cups green chili strips – thin
1 1/2 pounds grated Longhorn cheese
1 small diced brown onion
1/4 teaspoons diced garlic
3 tablespoons canola oil
2 cups evaporated canned milk
1 small can tomato sauce
2 cans chicken broth
4 cups water
Salt/pepper/garlic salt/onion salt to taste

1. In a medium size pot sauté onion and garlic in oil.
2. Add cubed potatoes and stir continuously for 5 minutes on medium heat.
3. Add broth and water to top of pot.
4. Add tomato sauce.
5. Add evaporated canned milk.
6. Cover and turn heat to medium low until potatoes are semi-soft.
7. Season with salt/pepper/ garlic salt/onion salt to taste.
8. Add chili and cheese on top of individual soup bowls when serving.

Casuela

Jerky

Ingredients:

3 cups dried carne seca meat
(dried jerky)

3 medium Russet potatoes;
peeled and cubed

2 tablespoons canola oil

1/4 cup green bell pepper

1/4 cup diced tomatoes

1/4 cup green onion

1/4 cup fresh

1 small can dice green chili

10 cups water

3 tablespoons; Knorr Caldo
deTomate powder

1/2 small can tomato sauce

Salt/pepper/garlic salt/onion
salt to taste

1. In a medium size cover pot sauté potatoes and meat in canola oil.

2. Add water.

3. Add Knorr Caldo de Tomate powder and stir.

4. Add tomato sauce.

5. Add vegetables.

6. Add green chili.

7. Season with salt/pepper/ onion salt/garlic salt to taste.

8. Cover and simmer on low for 45 minutes or until potatoes are semi-soft.

9. Serve and enjoy with warm flour tortillas (see page 165 for Flour Tortilla recipe).

Fideo

Vermicelli

Ingredients:
2 cups fideo noodles
1/3 cup canola oil
2 cans chicken broth
1/2 diced celery
2 cups shredded chicken
1 can of sliced carrots
1/2 cup chopped cilantro
    (or dried)
Water
Salt/pepper/garlic salt/
    onion salt to taste

1. In a medium sized pot; brown garlic and fideo in oil.
2. Add chicken broth.
3. Add water to fill pot.
4. Add celery.
5. Add chicken.
6. Add cilantro.
7. Cover and cook on medium low for 15 minutes.
8. Add carrots.
9. Season with salt/pepper/garlic salt/onion salt to taste.
10. Continue cooking on low for 10 minutes and serve.

Cocido

Vegetable Soup

Ingredients:

2 large Russet potatoes; peeled and diced in large cubes

1 large package large chucked meat (stew meat; boneless chuck or beef ribs)

1 small cubed brown onion

2 green zucchini cut in large cubes

2 cups fresh green beans

1 can rinsed garbanzo beans

3 medium carrot sticks; chunked

4 ears of corn (white or yellow) cut in 2-inch pieces

2 cans chicken broth

5 cups water

Salt/pepper/garlic salt/onion salt to taste

1. In a medium size pot boil meat until pink but not quite cooked.

2. Remove meat from pot and rinse off scum.

3. Pour water and broth into a large soup pot; add meat.

4. Add peeled and cubed potatoes.

5. Add onion; zucchini; green beans carrot and corn; cover and cook on medium low heat for 1 o 2 hours.

6. Add garbanzo beans; cook for half hour on medium until all vegetables are soft but semi-firm.

7. Season with salt/pepper/ garlic salt/onion salt to taste.

Menudo

Hominy and Tripe

Ingredients:

2 small bags of tripe and pig's feet

4 pounds clean mix tamal (looks like hominy, comes in a bag)

1 medium yellow onion

1 whole un-peeled garlic

2 1/2 gallons water

Salt/garlic salt/onion salt to taste

Condiments:

2 cups diced green onion

2 cups chopped cilantro

2 lemons cut into wedges

1/2 cup Chili Tepine

1. Wash tripas and remove excess grease.

2. Cut into small squares (pigs feet are optional can be added).

3. Add water into a large menudo pot.

4. Add whole peeled yellow onion.

5. Add whole un-peeled garlic.

6. Add mix tamal and boil for 1 hour.

7. Add tripe; cover and cook on medium heat for 4 hours or until mix tamal is semi-soft being careful not to overcook.

8. Season with salt/onion salt/garlic salt to taste.

9. Add condiments and serve on top of soup.

Posole Beef/Bean

Ingredients:

2 packages ox tail or boneless ribs

4 pounds clean mix tamal

4 cups pinto beans

2 cups chili paste

1 medium yellow onion

1 whole un-peeled garlic

2 1/2 gallons water in a large menudo pot

Salt/garlic salt/onion salt to taste

1. Add water into a large menudo.

2. Add whole peeled yellow onion.

3. Add 1 whole un-peeled garlic.

4. Add beans.

5. Add mix tamal.

6. Add meat; cover and cook on medium heat for 3 hours.

7. Remove scum on top and add chili paste.

8. Season with salt/garlic salt/onion salt to taste.

9. Cook another hour on medium high or until mix tamal is semi-soft (do not overcook).

Red Chili Sauce: Boil 6 large chili pods (hot or mild with veins and stems removed) in water. When the chili pods turn bright red and are soft, remove from heat then remove pods from water. Let them cool and place them in blender on (low or puree) with 2 garlic cloves. Use water from pods as needed for thinner texture and salt to taste.

Note: For a quickie you can use Santa Cruz Chili Paste and thin with water or broth.

Tortilla Soup with Chicken

Ingredients:

3 cups cooked white chicken
   shredded in large strips

3 cans chicken broth

3 cups water

2 diced Roma tomatoes diced

1 cup diced green onions

1 cup chopped cilantro

2 large avocados cut in small
   diced chunks

3 cups grated Longhorn
   cheese

1 small bag white corn tortilla
   strips

Salt/pepper/garlic salt/onion
   salt to taste

1. In a medium sized pot boil water and chicken broth.

2. Add chicken strips.

3. Add cilantro; green onions and tomatoes.

4. Cover and cook on medium for 20 minutes.

5. Season with salt/pepper/ garlic salt/onion salt to taste.

6. Serve each plate individually and add avocados; chips and cheese as desired.

Soups are so nourishing and easy to prepare. Use your imagination, if you prefer chicken over beef then the choice it yours! There is no concrete law that says you have to have beef or chicken or either in any of the soups or dishes use whatever you have or prefer. Shrimp makes great soups or any of your favorite white fish also works well. If you want to add tomato sauce you can or if you want a clear base broth that is perfectly acceptable. If you like mushrooms throw those in for variety.

Posole de Puerco

Ingredients:

8 pork pigs' feet (or pork pieces)
4 pounds clean mix tamal
2 cups chili paste
1 whole medium yellow onion
1 whole unpeeled garlic
2 1/2 gallons of water
Salt/garlic salt/onion salt to taste

Condiments:

2 cups diced yellow onion
2 lemons cut into wedges
1/2 cup oregano

1. Add water into a large menudo.
2. Add whole peeled brown onion.
3. Add whole un-peeled garlic.
4. Add mix tamal; boil for 1 hour.
5. Add chili.
6. Add meat; cover and cook on medium heat for 3 hours or until mix tamal is semi-soft (do not overcook).
7. Season with salt/garlic salt/onion salt to taste.
8. Add condiments and serve on top of soup.

Red Chili Sauce: Boil 6 large chili pods (hot or mild with veins and stems removed) in water. When the chili pods turn bright red and are soft, remove from heat then remove pods from water. Let them cool and place them in blender on (low or puree) with 2 garlic cloves. Use water from pods as needed for thinner texture and salt to taste.

 Note: For a quickie you can use Santa Cruz Chili Paste and thin with water or broth.

Vegetable Stew Soup

Ingredients:
1 pound cubed stew meat
3 Russet potatoes, cubed
1 cup sliced raw carrots
1 cup frozen green peas
1 1/2 pounds raw Brussels
   sprouts
1 small can tomato puree
1 can of stewed tomatoes
1 can yellow corn
1 teaspoon sugar
1 tablespoon pickling spice
1/2 cup flour
1/2 cup canola oil
10 cups water
Salt/pepper/garlic salt/onion
   salt to taste

1. Roll meat in flour and brown in oil in a medium size covered pot.
2. Add puree and simmer for 5 minutes.
3. Add stewed tomatoes.
4. Add water.
5. Add vegetables.
6. Add pickling spice.
7. Add corn.
8. Cover and let cook on medium low heat for 1 1/2 hours or until meat is tender.
9. Season with salt/pepper/onion salt/garlic salt to taste.

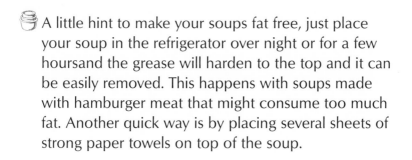 A little hint to make your soups fat free, just place your soup in the refrigerator over night or for a few hoursand the grease will harden to the top and it can be easily removed. This happens with soups made with hamburger meat that might consume too much fat. Another quick way is by placing several sheets of strong paper towels on top of the soup.

Vertholaga's (Greens)

Ingredients:

2 pounds clean vertholagas greens

5 cups water or enough water to cover vertholagas

1/3 cup diced garlic

1/4 cup diced brown onion

2 diced Roma tomatoes

3 tablespoons canola oil

2 tablespoons flour

1 cup milk

3 cups grated Longhorn cheese

Salt/pepper/garlic salt/onion salt to taste

1. In a medium size pot boil vertholagas for 15 minutes; add enough water to cover.

2. In a small skillet brown garlic and onion in oil.

3. Add flour to garlic and onion and brown.

4. Add milk to make a white sauce.

5. Drain vertholagas and add white sauce mixture and stir.

6. Add tomatoes.

7. Add cheese.

8. Season with salt/pepper/ garlic salt/onion salt to taste.

9. Stir all ingredients; if too thick, add more milk or water for a semi-thin soup consistency.

10. Cover and let simmer on low for 20 minutes.

Vertholagas are a very nutritious green that can either be bought in a grocery store (preferably a grocery store that caters to the Hispanic culture) or they can be picked in your own back yard. The green looks very similar to the pigweed but the leaves are much smaller. This dish is quite a delicacy in the Hispanic culture.

Tacos

A Taste of Love from the Heart

Ground Beef Patty Tacos

Ingredients:
1 pound lean ground beef
1 dozen thin corn tortillas
3 cups canola oil
Salt/pepper/garlic salt/onion
    to taste

Filling Ingredients:
1 small head thinly shredded
    lettuce
1/2 pound grated long horn
    cheese
1 small can mixed
    peas/carrots

Sauce for Tacos:
In a small bowl place 1 can of diced or whole tomatoes; squish thoroughly with your hands. Add 1/4 cup cilantro; 1/4 cup green onions; 1/2 teaspoon oregano; dash of salt/pepper/ garlic salt/ onion salt; 2 drops vinegar and stir well.

1. Season meat with salt/pepper/ garlic salt/onion salt; not too heavy as sauce has salt.

2. Place half a hamburger patty on one side of the tortilla.

3. In a large stainless steel skillet heat oil.

4. Place tortillas flat in oil until tortilla begins to harden; quickly fold half way over using tongs leaving a gap; cook one side then the other; gap is to place filling in the taco (tacos should be crispy not burnt).

5. Drain excess oil and standup in a loaf pan lined with a paper towel.

6. Fill tacos with sauce (see below) lettuce; mixed peas/ carrots; cheese and top with Red Thin Salsa for hot and spicy flavor. (See page 113 for Red Thin Salsa recipe.)

Ground Beef & Potato Tacos

Ingredients:
1 pound lean ground beef
2 brown Russet potatoes
1 dozen thin corn tortillas
4 cups canola oil
Salt/pepper/garlic salt/onion
    to taste

Filling Ingredients:
1/2 small head thinly
    shredded lettuce
1/2 pound grated Longhorn
    cheese
1 small can mixed
    peas/carrots
1/2 cup thinly sliced radishes

Sauce for Tacos:
In a small bowl place 1 can of diced or whole tomatoes; squish thoroughly with your hands. Add 1/4 cup cilantro; 1/4 cup green onions; 1/2 teaspoon oregano; dash of salt/pepper/garlic salt/ onion salt; 2 drops vinegar and stir well.

1. Boil potatoes until semi-soft (for a quickie use frozen diced hash browns).

2. Dice potatoes and brown in oil.

3. Season meat with salt/ pepper/garlic salt/onion salt; (not too heavy) as sauce has salt.

4. Fry meat with the potatoes (not too much oil).

5. In a large stainless steel skillet heat oil.

6. Place tortilla in oil until tortillas begins to harden; quickly fold half way over using tongs leaving a gap; cook one side then the other; gap is to place filling in the taco (tacos should be crispy not burnt).

7. Drain excess oil and standup in a loaf pan lined with a paper towel.

8. Fill tacos with meat mixture; sauce (see below) lettuce; mixed peas/carrots; radishes; cheese and top with Thin Red Salsa for hot and spicy flavor. (See page 113 for Red Thin Salsa recipe.)

Rolled Chicken Tacos

Ingredients
1 package skinned chicken
   parts
1 dozen thin corn tortillas
3 cups canola oil
Salt/pepper to taste

Filling Ingredients:
1/2 small head thinly
   shredded lettuce
1/2 pound grated Longhorn
   cheese
1 small can mixed
   peas/carrots

Sauce for Tacos:
In a small bowl place 1 can of
diced or whole tomatoes;
squish thoroughly with your
hands. Add 1/4 cup cilantro;
1/4 cup green onions;
1/2 teaspoon oregano; dash
of salt; pepper; garlic salt and
onion salt; 2 drops vinegar
and stir well.

1. Boil chicken parts in
   boiling water until fully
   cooked and tender; let
   cool.
2. Shred chicken and season
   with salt/pepper to taste.
3. Place a few strips of
   chicken on one side of the
   tortilla and roll.
4. Heat oil in a large stainless
   steel skillet.
5. Use tongs to hold taco
   together and place in oil
   until tortilla is crispy;
   quickly turn over with
   tongs and fry the other
   side.
6. Drain excess oil and stand
   up in a loaf pan lined with
   a paper towel.
7. Top tacos with sauce; (see
   below) lettuce, mixed
   peas/ carrots; cheese and
   top with Thin Red Salsa for
   hot and spicy flavor. (See
   page 113 for Red Thin
   Salsa recipe.)

Notes

Tamales

Bean Tamales

Ingredients:
2 pounds masa
1/4 cup salt (or to taste)
1 package dried tamale
    leaves (hojas)
1 quart water

Filling:
3 cups cooked whole pinto
    beans
1 cup dark raisins
2 large cone brown sugar
    (pilonzio)
2 cups water
1 teaspoon cinnamon
1/2 teaspoon cloves

1. In a slow cooker cook beans until soft yet keep their form (approximately 4 hours on high).

2. Drain beans and cool.

3. In a medium pot add 2 cups water and 2 cones of brown sugar (pilonzio); boil constantly stirring to a thick and syrup like consistency.

4. Place beans in a blender until smooth and remove.

5. In a medium bowl add beans; raisins; cloves; cinnamon.

6. Slowly add syrup into the bean mixture until it reaches a jam-like texture.

A Taste of Love from the Heart

Peparing/Cooking Bean Tamales

1. Place tamale leaf (hoja) with pointed end up and spread masa semi-thin across leaf 1/2-inch from bottom of tamale leaf (hoja) and 2 inches from top; same as plastering (see pictures on pages 160 and 161). The white tool shown in the picture or flat spatula works well for spreading.

2. Place 1 tablespoon bean mixture to left of leaf on masa.

3. Roll to the right and fold top of leaf down and place on tray.

4. Fill tamale steamer or pot with 1 quart water and stand tamales up; get damp kitchen cloth and place on top of tamales to retain moisture.

5. Cook on medium heat for 1 to 1 1/2 hours.

6. Test 1 tamale by removing from the pot and let cool to form and take shape; taste to see if thoroughly cooked.

Green Corn Tamales

Ingredients:

2 1/2 dozen white corn
Leaves (hojas) from corn, cleaned
2 pounds lard or shortening
2 pounds small curd cottage cheese
1 pound grated Jack cheese
4 pounds fresh green chili (strips)
2 pounds grated Longhorn cheese
1 can evaporated milk (if needed)
1 cup sugar
1/4 cup salt

1. Remove hard core of corn
2. Remove leaves; clean and save.
3. Remove hair from corn.
4. Use electric knife to remove kernels from cob and store in plastic freezer bags.
5. Take corn to be stone ground at a Tortilla Factory.
6. In a large tamale mixing tub; whip lard with electric mixer for 3 minutes (like whipping cream).
7. Pour in the ground corn.
8. Pour in cottage cheese.
9. Add Longhorn cheese.
10. Slowly pour in milk mixing to a semi-thick) consistently using your hands to blend ingredients thoroughly.

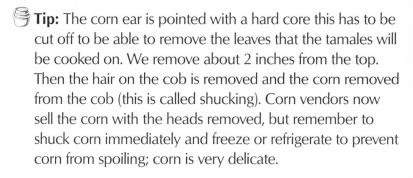 **Tip:** The corn ear is pointed with a hard core this has to be cut off to be able to remove the leaves that the tamales will be cooked on. We remove about 2 inches from the top. Then the hair on the cob is removed and the corn removed from the cob (this is called shucking). Corn vendors now sell the corn with the heads removed, but remember to shuck corn immediately and freeze or refrigerate to prevent corn from spoiling; corn is very delicate.

A Taste of Love from the Heart

Green Chili Tamale Meat

1. Rub cooking oil on 4 large tomatoes and roast in the oven at 400 degrees until soft & toasty.

2. 1 pound green roasted chili strips (store bought or roast same as tomatoes).

3. Cube 2 pounds beef stew meat or boneless cross rib into small pieces.

4. Dice 2 fresh garlic cloves.

5. Roll meat in flour and brown with garlic in 1/4 cup oil on medium heat in a skillet.

6. Add roasted tomatoes and mash.

7. Add green chili strips.

8. Add 3/4 cup water.

9. Season with salt/pepper/garlic salt/onion salt to taste.

10. Stir meat mixture which will be a gravy-like consistency.

A Taste of Love from the Heart

Preparing/Cooking Green Corn Tamales

1. Place tamale leaf (hoja) with pointed end up.
2. Place one large cooking spoon of corn mixture to the left of the leaf (hoja) and 1/2-inch from the bottom of the leaf (hoja).
3. Place 3 strips of chili on top of mixture.
4. Place 1 teaspoon Longhorn grated cheese on top of chili.
5. Roll leaf (hoja) to the right and fold top of leaf (hoja) down.
6. Place rolled tamales on a tray or place in freezer bags (1 dozen or 1/2 dozen).
7. Fill tamale steamer or pot with 8 cups water and stand tamales up on rack being careful not to let tamales touch the water.
8. Get a damp clean kitchen cloth and place over the tamales to retain the moisture.
9. Cook on medium heat for 1 to 1 1/2 hours.
10. Test 1 tamale by removing from the pot and let cool to form and take shape; taste to see if thoroughly cooked.

Green corn tamales can be very tedious to make and very hard work if you want to produce a large quantity. I have found that if you make a small amount as my recipe, you will not tire yourself out and it does not require a whole day's work. I am very proud of this recipe; I took first place three years in a row in the Tucson City Contest for the best tasting tamales. My youngest son wanted to earn money for car insurance and decided to make tamales to raise the money. I volunteered to do the preparing if he did the labor cleaning and shucking 30 dozen corn. Needless to say it was a whole weekend project and he appreciated the work it took in making and preparing the green corn tamales.

Red Chili Beef Tamales

Ingredients:
20 pounds masa
4 bags of dried leaves (hojas)
3 1/2 pounds lard (or
   shortening
3 3/4 cup suet fat (Manteca
   de Res)
2 cups red chili sauce
6 cups beef broth
1/3 cup salt

1. In a large tamale mixing tub; whip lard with electric mixer for 3 minutes (like whipping cream).
2. Add masa and salt.
3. Add suet fat and chili sauce.
4. Add broth use (little at a time to semi-thick consistency).
5. Use hands to blend ingredients thoroughly.

Red Chili Tamale Meat

Ingredients:
2 boneless cross rib roasts
1 large pork roast
3/4 cup canola oil
2 tablespoons of diced garlic
3 cups red chili sauce
Salt/onion salt/garlic salt to taste
1 medium bottle Spanish green olives (will be used when preparing tamales)

1. In a large pot boil cross rib roast on medium low for 3 hours or until tender but does not fall apart.
2. Boil pork roast same as beef.
3. Let meat cool and dice in small cubes.
4. Place oil in pot and sauté garlic.
5. Add cubed meat.
6. Add chili sauce and stir.
7. Season with salt/garlic salt/onion salt to taste.
8. Simmer on medium low heat for 1 hour.

A Taste of Love from the Heart

Preparing/Cooking Red Chili Tamales

1. Place tamale leaf (hoja) with pointed end up and spread masa semi-thin across leaf 1/2-inch from bottom of tamale leaf (hoja) and 2 inches from top; same as plastering (see pictures on pages 160 and 161). The white tool shown in the picture or flat spatula works well for spreading.

2. Place 1 tablespoon meat to left of leaf on masa and add 1 Spanish olive.

3. Roll to the right and fold top of leaf down; place on tray.

4. Fill tamale steamer or pot with 1 quart of water and stand tamales up; get damp kitchen cloth and place on top of tamales to retain moisture.

5. Cook on medium heat for 1 to 1 1/2 hours.

6. Test 1 tamale by removing from the pot and let cool to form and take shape; taste to see if thoroughly cooked.

As the boys were growing up, this became a Christmas project. The boys in the neighborhood would pitch in and help (Cris, Cliff, Diego and Gavino). We worked well as a team. All the boys helped with tortilla kneading, bean mashing, tamale making, baking cookies and barbeque grilling. After a hard days work we would end the day by taking a dip in our pool and relaxing. The neighborhood boys would either sleep over or swim into the night playing and horsing around. These days remain priceless to me and will always bring about fond memories. Gavino has since left us to be with the Lord, but will always be remembered.

Tortillas & Breads

Flour Tortillas

Ingredients:
4 cups flour
1/3 cup lard or shortening
1/3 cup salt
1 1/2 cups warm water

1. In a large bowl combine flour; salt and lard.
2. Add water slowly; if needed add more water.
3. Work dough until soft not sticky.
4. Roll into medium balls.
5. Place on a cookie sheet and press down on each.
6. Cover with clean kitchen towel and let stand for 1 hour.
7. Use rolling pin to roll out dough; continue to stretch with hands to medium round size.
8. Cook on hot flat cast iron grill. In Spanish this is referred to as a "placa." (see pictures of placa on page 164).

Gordita Tortillas

Ingredients:
5 pounds flour
2 cups shortening
3 tablespoons salt
2/3 cup sugar
3 cans evaporated milk
3/4 cup cold water

1. In a large bowl mix flour; salt and shortening.
2. Add milk.
3. Work dough until soft not sticky.
4. Add water slowly; if needed; add more water.
5. Roll into medium balls with greased hands.
6. Place in an air tight container.
7. Let stand for 1 hour.
8. Use rolling pin to roll out dough into small round size.
9. Cook on hot flat cast iron grill; "placa." (see pictures of placa on pages 164).
10. Press down on the edges of the tortilla with a potholder while cooking.

Yeast Bread

Ingredients:
6 cups flour
1 1/2 cups shortening
1/8 cup salt
2 1/3 cups warm water
2 packages of dry yeast

1. In a large mixing bowl pour in flour.
2. Add shortening.
3. Add salt.
4. Mix and remove all lumps.
5. In a small bowl mix water and dry yeast; add slowly and stir.
6. Pour into flour mixture and mix well.
7. Grease hands and make small balls with dough.
8. Lay balls on a cookie sheet; press down on each gently with a fork.
9. Cover with clean kitchen towel for 2 hours and let rise.
10. Bake in pre-heated oven at 350 degrees for 30 minutes or until golden brown.

Homemade yeast bread and chili beans—yummy, yummy, yummy, in the tummy, tummy, tummy! Nanie's favorite saying to the grandbabies. There is nothing like the aroma of yeast bread cooking in the oven. These are fond memories that are priceless!

Mexican Corn Bread

Ingredients:

1 can or box plain corn bread mix

2 cans diced green chili; drained

1 small block Velveeta cheese

1 can cream corn

1. Follow instructions on corn bread box and prepare accordingly.

2. Add 1 can cream corn.

3. On a greased square glass dish pour half the corn mixture and spread evenly.

4. Spread a layer of green chilies.

5. Spread a layer of sliced cheese.

6. Pour remaining corn mixture on top.

7. Bake in pre-heated oven at 350 degrees for 30 minutes or until golden brown (check with a toothpick) to make sure corn bread is fully cooked.

Traditional
Turkey Dinner

172 Traditional Turkey Dinner

Candied Yams

Ingredients:

3 small fresh peeled yams
1 cup chopped pecans
1/2 cup margarine
1 cup brandy
1 cup spiced rum
1 1/2 cups dark brown sugar

1. Boil fresh yams for 1 hour or until soft.
2. Place yams in a glass dish.
3. In a sauce pan brown pecans in margarine.
4. Add brandy; rum and stir.
5. Pour over yams.
6. Place in a 400 degree pre-heated oven for 2 hours or until yams are tender and dark brown.
7. Add marshmallows the last 5 minutes of baking and brown under broiler until marshmallows have toasted.

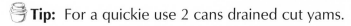 **Tip:** For a quickie use 2 cans drained cut yams.

Fresh Smashed Yams

Ingredients:
3 large fresh yams
1 cup margarine
1 cup light corn syrup
Salt/pepper to taste

1. Wash yams; slit with knife on top of each.
2. Place in microwave for 25 minutes or until soft.
3. Slice yams with a long knife.
4. Scoop out yam filling and place in a medium bowl.
5. Add margarine and mix.
6. Add light corn syrup.
7. Salt and pepper to taste.

French Style Green Bean Casserole

Ingredients:
1 large bag frozen French cut green beans
1 can cream of mushroom soup
1 cup canned French fried onions
3/4 cup milk
Salt/pepper to taste

1. In a small sauce pan stir mushroom soup and milk.
2. Add green beans.
3. Salt/pepper to taste.
4. Place in a glass dish.
5. Place onions on top of green beans.
6. Bake in a 350 degree pre- heated oven for 30 minutes.

Fresh Mashed Potatoes

Ingredients:
4 large brown Russet
   potatoes
1 stick of butter
1 cup evaporated milk
Salt/pepper to taste

1. Slice 1/3-inch peeled Russet potatoes.
2. Boil sliced potatoes in a medium covered pot until soft.
3. Drain out water.
4. Add butter.
5. Add evaporated milk.
6. Mix at medium speed for 3 minutes or until creamy.
7. Add salt/pepper to taste.

Stuffing

Carrillo Traditional Dressing

Ingredients:
1 box Yellow Corn Meal*
1 bag toasted bread pieces
3 cubes of butter
3 potatoes peeled, boiled and
    mashed
2 turkey drumsticks
2 tablespoons oregano
Dash of sage
1 package corn stuffing mix
1 cup diced celery
1 cup diced green onions
1 cup green bell pepper
Boiled diced gizzards
Salt/pepper to taste

*make 1 recipe of cornbread
from Albers Yellow Corn
Meal according to directions
on package and set aside

1. In a large deep pot melt butter.

2. Add vegetables.

3. Add gizzards and shredded meat from drumsticks (set aside 1 cup for gravy).

4. Add toasted bread and stuffing mix.

5. Crumble cooled cornbread (reserve 1 cup aside to sprinkle on top).

6. Add potatoes.

7. Add oregano.

8. Sprinkle dash of sage (this spice can be very over-powering).

9. Add broth to soft texture.

10. Salt/pepper to taste.

11. Spread mixture on a large rectangular dish; sprinkle cornbread and butter on top.

A Taste of Love from the Heart

My grandparents had a ranch hand cook who prepared most of the meals for the workers. His name was Julian Bush, nicknamed "Duke". He taught Grandma Carrillo how to make what is now known as the "traditional Carrillo dressing." Individual methods have been used by family members in preparing this dish such as some use diced potatoes, others rice them, and yet others mash them, but they all work according to your preference. The basic recipe isn't compromised; it's just a personal preference, but remains a family tradition!

I have made alterations, but the basics still apply. This recipe goes a long ways, so you may want to decrease ingredients equally, if it is for a small meal.

This recipe was Dad's favorite and he looked forward to the big meal. Fortunately, Dad was able to have his last big Thanksgiving dinner in 1992, just a few days before he passed away. Thanksgiving will always be a special day in my heart.

Picadillo Dressing

Avila Thanksgiving Tradition

Ingredients:

1 pound lean hamburger
  meat
1/2 cup diced brown onion
1/4 cup diced celery
1/4 cup diced carrots
1/4 cup dark raisins (optional)
1/4 cup diced apples
  (optional)
1 small can sliced black olives
2 cups sherry wine
1/4 teaspoon sugar
1/4 teaspoon cinnamon
1/4 teaspoon salt
1/4 teaspoon pepper
1/4 teaspoon onion salt
Dash of powdered cloves

1. In a large skillet, fry meat.
2. Add vegetables and olives.
3. Add raisins and apples.
4. Add wine.
5. Add sugar.
6. Add cinnamon.
7. Add salt.
8. Add pepper.
9. Add onion salt.
10. Add a dash of cloves.
11. Simmer on low for
    30 minutes.

Dough for Fried Empanadas (Turnovers): Mix 3 cups flour; 1/2 cup shortening; 1 1/2 tablespoons salt and 1 cup cold water; work until dough is soft and not sticky (add more water if needed); roll small golf balls of dough into round circles; add Picadillo filling on one side of circle and fold in half; turn and pinch edges over to lock (like a pie) and fry in hot oil until golden brown.

Turkey

Ingredients:
1 small 15-pound turkey
Salt/pepper to taste
Soft margarine
1 cup melted margarine to
    inject in turkey

1. Place turkey in an aluminum turkey pan.

2. Sprinkle salt/pepper on both sides of turkey.

3. Spread margarine all over turkey.

4. Mix pre-heated margarine with herb and garlic marinade.

5. Inject margarine into turkey legs; thighs and breasts.

6. Cover turkey with heavy duty tin foil tightly.

7. Place in a 250 degree oven for 8 hours (for those turkeys with a red button inserted, button will pop up when cooked.

8. Turn oven up to 475 degrees; remove tin foil from top and let turkey brown until golden.

Other Traditional items include: Sliced cranberry sauce; hot bread rolls; pumpkin pie (see Pumpkin/Lemon Pie (Carrillo Thanksgiving Tradition on page 210) and homemade apple pie (see Apple Pie – A Family Thanksgiving Tradition on page 185).

Turkey Gravy

Ingredients:
2 sticks butter
Turkey drippings
1 cup water
1/4 cup corn starch
1/3 teaspoon poultry
   seasoning
1/3 teaspoon powdered sage

Salt/pepper to taste
1 cup shredded turkey and
   gizzards

1. Strain turkey drippings into a medium pot.
2. Use a shaker (with wheel) to mix corn starch and water; shake until thin texture with no lumps.
3. Add to drippings and stir.
4. Add sage and poultry seasoning.
5. Add 1 cup shredded turkey meat with gizzards.
6. Stir constantly until texture is smooth and semi-thin.

Notes

Desserts

Apple Pie

A Family Thanksgiving Tradition

Ingredients:
1 box piecrust mix
8 peeled green apples
1 1/2 cups sugar
1 stick margarine
1/2 cup cinnamon
1/2 cup nutmeg
1/3 cup cloves

1. Prepare piecrust according to package directions.
2. Peel and slice apples.
3. Lay piecrust on a large deep pie tin.
4. Place a layer of apples on crust.
5. Place thin slices of margarine evenly.
6. Sprinkle heavy layer of sugar.
7. Sprinkle cinnamon.
8. Sprinkle nutmeg.
9. Sprinkle cloves lightly.
10. Repeat layers.
11. Lay top crust and roll edges; poke with fork.
12. Coat top of crust with milk or white egg wash and sprinkle sugar and cinnamon on top.
13. Bake in pre-heated oven at 350 degrees for 45 minutes (check apples with a knife).

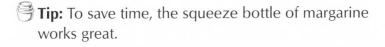 **Tip:** To save time, the squeeze bottle of margarine works great.

Brownies

A Family Christmas Tradition

Ingredients:
1 1/2 cups flour
1 1/2 cups sugar
1 cup shortening
4 eggs
1/2 cup cocoa
1/2 cup chopped walnuts
 (optional)
2 teaspoons vanilla
Dash of salt

1. In a large bowl combine flour; sugar and shortening.
2. Add beaten eggs.
3. Add vanilla.
4. Add Hershey's powdered cocoa
5. Add salt
6. Add nuts (optional) and stir well
7. Spread in a greased 9 x 9-inch glass dish
8. Bake in pre-heated oven at 350 degrees for 25 minutes (check with a toothpick) to make sure brownies are fully cooked.

Banana Nut Bread

Ingredients:
1 3/4 cup flour
2 eggs
1/3 cup shortening
1/2 cup sugar
1/2 teaspoon baking soda
1/2 teaspoon salt
1/2 teaspoon baking powder
1 1/2 teaspoons mashed ripe
   bananas
1 cup chopped nuts

1. Beat together shortening; sugar and eggs at low speed.

2. Add flour; baking soda; salt and baking powder and blend.

3. Add bananas and nuts and stir.

4. Pour into a large greased loaf pan.

5. Bake in pre-heated oven at 350 degrees for 45 minutes (check with a toothpick) to make sure bread is fully cooked.

During my elementary years of school, mom would always make this pie for our lunches. She used to make the pie on a cookie sheet and would cut each individual piece in squares, so that she could bag and freeze the portions. The only exception to my mother's recipe is that she used a homemade pie crust, which takes much longer to prepare. With time being of the essence in our busy lives, we can still enjoy the great eminent flavors of these splendid recipes. The wonderful smell of banana bread filled the house and the anxiety of waiting until it was ready to eat. Mom would pour the batter into small greased tin juice cans. She would cool them off and slice them into circles and serve them with cream cheese—what a treat!

Buenellos

Fried Tortillas with Syrup
(A Family New Year's Tradition)

Ingredients:
5 pounds self-rising flour
Water
1 dozen eggs
1/4 cup salt
1/4 cup shortening
1 gallon of canola oil

1. In a large bowl combine flour and eggs.
2. Slowly add in water as needed.
3. Add salt.
4. Roll in to medium size balls and grease the top of each.
5. Stretch dough out to medium tortilla size; fry in hot oil until golden on both sides.
6. Drain standing up in a tin pan lined with paper towels.

Syrup: In a medium saucepan combine 2 pounds cone shaped brown sugar (pilonzio) or you can use brown sugar and 4 cups water; add 3 cinnamon sticks on medium heat. Stir mixture to a semi-thin syrup consistency. Pour syrup lightly on top of buenellos or you can substitute with cinnamon and sugar sprinkled on top.

Buenellos are a traditional New Year's treat that are eaten with syrup or cinnamon and sugar. This was Grandma Carrillo's recipe, given to me by my cousin Baby Alice. I spent the day with her learning how to prepare and make this tradition. Alice, I thank you and God rest your soul, you left us too early. You were supposed to join us for Jimmy's big 21 birthday celebration and instead you left that day on your journey.

Capirotada
Bread Pudding

Ingredients:

1 loaf toasted dry bread

2 cups brown sugar or cone brown sugar (pilonzio - 2)

1 cup peanuts or walnuts

2 cups peeled apple slices

2 cups bananas (optional)

1/2 cup cilantro

1/2 cup diced green onion

2 cups Longhorn or Colby cheese

2 sticks melted butter

1 teaspoon cinnamon

1 teaspoon nutmeg

1/2 teaspoon cloves

1 teaspoon vanilla

1. Toast bread or buy in a bag.

2. Heat 2 cups water with brown sugar.

3. Add cinnamon; nutmeg and cloves to sugar and stir.

4. Add vanilla and stir.

5. In large bowl mix bread; cilantro; green onion; melted butter; nuts and apples (bananas optional).

6. Add hot brown sugar mixture and stir.

7. Spread one layer of bread mixture on large glass dish top with cheese and repeat.

8. Bake in pre-heated oven at 350 degrees for 1 hour or until golden brown.

9. Let cool and serve.

Capirotada is a sacred dessert served all during the period of Lent. This dish as well as lentil beans is considered a holy meal and is observed by the Hispanic culture during the period of 40 weekdays before Easter. Catholic and Christian churches all over the world regard this period as a time of prayer, penance, fasting and self-denial.

Lime Cheesecake

Ingredients:
3 eggs
3/4 cup water
3/4 cup sugar
1 envelope unflavored gelatin
1/4 cup cold water
1 cup cream
8 ounces cream cheese
1/4 cup lime juice
1 teaspoon grated lime rind
2 drops green food coloring

Crust:
5 large graham crackers
1 tablespoon sugar
1 tablespoon melted margarine

1. Press graham cracker mixture down in a 9-inch spring form pan and refrigerate 1 hour.

2. Dissolve gelatin in 1/4 cup cold water.

3. In a medium pot combine 3 egg yolks; water; sugar; stir for 5 minutes over medium heat.

4. Add gelatin mixture; cream cheese; lime juice; lime rind and food coloring.

5. Fold in cream and beaten egg whites.

6. Pour into crust and refrigerate 1 hour and serve.

I use to make this recipe for my father when I was still living at home. He loved cheese cake, but unfortunately in 1974 he had open heart surgery and he had to eliminate cheese, sugar and eggs from his diet due to high cholesterol and diabetes. This is an easy and tasty recipe to prepare.

Carrot Cake

Ingredients:
2 cups flour
2 cups sugar
3/4 teaspoon salt
2 teaspoons baking soda
2 teaspoons cinnamon
1 cup canola oil
4 beaten eggs
3 cups grated carrots
1 cup strained crushed
 pineapple
1 cup walnuts
3/4 cup coconut

Frosting Ingredients:
1 box powder sugar
3/4 cup margarine
8 ounce cream cheese
1 teaspoon vanilla
1/4 cup crushed nuts (top of
 frosting)

1. In a large bowl combine flour; sugar; salt; cinnamon and baking soda.

2. Add oil; eggs; carrots and pineapple.

3. Add nuts and coconut.

4. Beat on low speed until well blended.

5. Grease 3 small loaf pans and line with waxed paper.

6. Pour equal amounts of batter into pans.

7. Bake in pre-heated oven at 350 degrees for 1 hour (check with a toothpick) to make sure cake is fully cooked.

8. Mix frosting ingredients.

9. Let cake cool for 20 minutes and frost.

Chocolate Cream Tart

Ingredients:

1 cup flour
1 stick margarine
1/2 cup walnuts
1 large package cream
   cheese
1 large Cool Whip topping
3 cups milk
1 cup powdered sugar
2 small packages chocolate
   instant pudding mix (can
   substitute flavors)

1. In a large bowl combine flour; butter and nuts.

2. Press mixture down in an 8 x 8-inch glass dish.

3. Bake in pre-heated oven at 350 degrees for 15 minutes and let crust cool.

4. First Layer: Spread 1 cup Cool Whip on crust.

5. Mix remaining Cool Whip with cream cheese and powdered sugar.

6. Second Layer: Spread mixture on top of Cool Whip.

7. Third Layer: Spread remaining Cool Whip on top of cream cheese mixture.

8. Sprinkle top layer with nuts.

Chocolate Chip Cookies

A Family Christmas Tradition

Ingredients:
2 1/4 cups flour
1 teaspoon baking soda
    mixed in 1/2 tablespoon
    water
1 teaspoon salt
1 cup shortening
3/4 cup sugar
3/4 cup brown sugar
1 teaspoon vanilla extract
1 (12-ounce) package
    chocolate chip morsels
    (equals 2 cups)
1 cup walnuts

1. In large bowl combine flour; sugar; brown sugar; shortening; and salt.

2. Add baking soda mixture.

3. Add vanilla.

4. Add chocolate chips.

5. Add nuts and mix well.

6. Drop 1 teaspoon of dough on an un-greased cookie sheet; makes about 3 dozen.

7. Bake in pre-heated oven at 350 degrees for 10 minutes; cool on racks.

Empanadas — Turnovers

A Family Christmas Tradition

Ingredients:
2 boxes ready mix pie crust
1 large can pumpkin
1/2 tablespoon cinnamon
1/2 tablespoon nutmeg
1/2 tablespoon allspice
1/2 teaspoon cloves
2 tablespoons vanilla
Add 3 eggs
2 cups sugar
1 large cut and seal tool or a
    donut cutter

1. Cut pumpkin into squares and boil until soft.
2. Spoon out pumpkin from peel.
3. In a large pot combine sugar; cinnamon; nutmeg; allspice; and cloves.
4. Add beaten eggs.
5. Add vanilla.
6. Cook for 20 minutes stirring constantly.
7. Refrigerate for 2 hours.
8. Roll out crust.
9. Make small circles with a round cutter.
10. Add 1 teaspoon in center of dough and fold in half.
11. Use a cut and seal tool to seal edges or twist edges up by hand.
12. Use egg white or milk on top of each turnover.
13. Sprinkle each turnover lightly with cinnamon and sugar.
14. Bake in pre-heated oven at 350 degrees for 10 minutes or until golden brown.

Frosting for Cake Decorating

Ingredients:

1 pound plus 1/8 cup
   shortening
3 cups powdered sugar
1/2 cup water
1 teaspoon vanilla
Dash of salt

1. In a medium size mixing bowl beat shortening till fluffy.

2. Add powdered sugar.

3. Add water.

4. Add vanilla

5. Add salt.

6. Mix with electric beater at high speed for 2 minutes.

Harvey Wall-banger Cake

Ingredients:

1 box orange cake mix
1 small box 3.75-ounce
    instant vanilla pudding
5 eggs
1/2 cup canola oil
1/2 cup orange juice
1/2 cup Galliano Wine
2 caps Vodka

1. In a large bowl combine cake mix; pudding; and oil.
2. Add eggs.
3. Add Galliano wine.
4. Add orange juice.
5. Add Vodka.
6. Beat on low speed until blended.
7. Pour into a 10-inch bundt cake pan.
8. Bake in pre-heated oven at 350 degrees for 30 minutes (check with a toothpick) to make sure cake is fully cooked.
9. Cool for 15 minutes.
10. Remove cake from bundt pan.
11. Prepare frosting and drizzle over bundt cake.

Frosting

Combine 1 cup powdered sugar;1 tablespoon orange juice;1 tablespoon Galliano wine;1 teaspoon Vodka and mix well.

Jell-O Soufflé

Ingredients:
2 large black cherry Jell-O
6 tablespoons sugar
3 cups boiling water
6 cups crushed ice
2 (8-ounce) packages cream
    cheese

1. In a blender combine Jell-O; sugar; boiling water; let steam release.
2. Cover and blend on low for 1 minute.
3. Add cream cheese.
4. Add crushed ice.
5. Cover and blend at high speed for 2 minutes.
6. Pour into a plastic covered container.

Tip: Serve with Cool Whip and black cherries; makes a great presentation and tastes great!

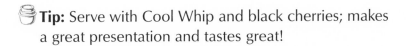

Orange Jell-O Whip

Ingredients:
1 large orange Jell-O
2 small containers Cool Whip
2 small containers small curd
    cottage cheese
2 small cans Mandarin
    oranges; drained
1/2 cup finely chopped nuts

1. In a large mixing bowl combine all ingredients and pour into a covered container.
2. Refrigerate for 1 hour and serve.

Oatmeal Crisps

Ingredients:
1 1/2 cups flour
1 cup butter flavored
   shortening
1 cup brown sugar
1 cup sugar
3 cups quick cook oatmeal
1/2 cup chopped nuts
2 eggs
1 teaspoon vanilla
1 teaspoon baking soda
1 teaspoon salt
1 cup baby chocolate chips
   (optional)

1. In a medium size bow combine: cream shortening; sugar; eggs and vanilla.

2. Add flour; salt and baking soda.

3. Stir in oats; nuts and chips.

4. Form into small balls.

5. Bake in pre-heated oven at 350 degrees for 11 minutes; let cool.

Peanut Butter Cookies

Ingredients:
1 1/4 cups flour
1/4 cup butter
1/4 cup shortening
1/2 cup peanut butter
1/2 cup sugar
1/2 cup brown sugar
1 egg
3/4 teaspoon baking soda
1/2 teaspoon baking powder
1/4 teaspoon salt

1. In a medium bowl combine flour; butter and shortening.
2. Add peanut butter and stir.
3. Add sugar; brown sugar; egg; baking soda; baking powder and salt.
4. Bake in pre-heated oven at 350 degrees for 20 minutes or until golden brown.

This peanut butter cookie recipe has been in the family since I was in elementary school. I think this was one of the first recipes I ever made alone. When I was very young, Mom was hospitalized and I remember staying home from school and making these cookies to be able to take her a gift. What a proud feeling it gave me!

Pecan Tarts

A Family Christmas Tradition

Shell Ingredients:

1/2 pound margarine

2 (3-ounce) packages cream
  cheese

2 cups flour

1. In a medium bowl combine flour; cream cheese and butter.

2. In a small bowl combine pecans; melted butter; eggs; brown sugar; vanilla and salt.

3. Roll out dough into semi-thin circles (use a doughnut cutter for shape).

4. Place circles in muffin tea pans (mini muffin pans) and curl edges.

5. Place 1 teaspoon filling mixture in each tart.

6. Place 1 half slice of a pecan on each tart (great presentation). Bake in pre-heated oven at 350 degrees for 25 minutes or until golden brown.

7. Cool for 2 minutes and remove from tins.

A Taste of Love from the Heart

Filling

Ingredients:
1 cup chopped pecans
2 tablespoon melted
    margarine
2 eggs
4 drops vanilla
1 pinch of salt
1 1/2 cups light brown sugar

1. In a small bowl add chopped pecan.
2. Add melted margarine.
3. Add 2 eggs.
4. Add vanilla and a pinch of salt.
5. Add light brown sugar and mix well.

This recipe was given to me by my brother-in-law's (Bob Gabriel) mother. The pecan tarts are everybody's favorite Christmas treat. Bob was taken on his journey at a very young age with his mother following shortly after. I always enjoyed Bob's company and interesting stories. Thank you Mrs. Gabriel for sharing this great recipe and may you both rest in peace.

Pineapple Tapioca Pudding

Ingredients:
1 quart fresh milk
4 tablespoons tapioca
3/4 cup sugar
1 teaspoon vanilla
3 eggs
3 tablespoons cornstarch
1 small bag miniature
    marshmallows
1 can drained crushed
    pineapple
Cinnamon to taste

1. In a medium size pot heat milk slowly to a boil.
2. Add tapioca; vanilla and sugar stirring constantly.
3. Separate egg whites and beat until stiff and set aside.
4. Use a shaker (with wheel) to mix corn starch and egg yolks.
5. Pour mixture into hot milk stirring constantly until it thickens.
6. Place egg whites into a medium size covered bowl and fold in hot mixture.
7. Add drained crushed pineapple; marshmallows and stir.
8. Sprinkle with cinnamon; cover and refrigerate.

Pineapple Upside Down Cake

Ingredients:
1 pound can of sliced
    pineapple
1 yellow boxed cake mix with
    pudding added
5 eggs
1 vanilla instant pudding
1/2 cup oil
1/2 stick of melted margarine
1 cup pineapple juice
2 cups light brown sugar
Maraschino cherries
1 cup pecan halves

1. Melt margarine and spread in pan.

2. Arrange sliced pineapples with cherries in hole on pan greased with margarine.

3. Spread pecans around the empty areas of the pineapple slices.

4. Sprinkle brown sugar on top to cover pineapples/cherries.

5. Combine in a medium size bowl cake mix; eggs; pudding; oil and juice; mix at high speed.

6. Pour cake mixture over the pineapple slices, cherries and nuts.

7. Bake in pre-heated oven at 350 degrees for 45 minutes or until golden brown (check with a toothpick) to make sure cake is fully cooked.

Pistachio Nut Cake

Ingredients:
1 box white cake mix
1/2 cup milk
1/2 cup water
1/2 cup canola oil
6 eggs
2 small boxes pistachio
    instant pudding
1 cup chopped walnuts

1. In a large bowl combine cake mix; pudding and oil.
2. Add eggs, water and oil.
3. Add nuts.
4. Add 2 small boxes instant pudding.
5. Beat on low speed until blended.
6. Grease 3 small cake pans and line with waxed paper.
7. Pour batter into pans with equal amounts.
8. Bake in pre-heated oven at 350 degrees for 45 minutes or until golden brown (check with a toothpick) to make sure cake is fully cooked.
9. Cool for 20 minutes.

A Taste of Love from the Heart

Frosting

Ingredients:
10 tablespoons flour
1 cup milk
2 cup sugar
1 pound margarine
1 teaspoon vanilla
1 small box Jell-O pistachio
   instant pudding
1/2 cup chopped walnuts

1. Use a shaker (with wheel) to combine flour and milk and shake vigorously.

2. Cook mixture in a pre-heated pot stirring constantly until it thickens; cool in fridge for 10 minutes.

3. Beat margarine; sugar and vanilla and 1 small box instant pudding for 2 minutes at low speed; add flour and milk mixture and whip at high speed for 3 minutes.

4. Spread on each layer of cake and sides and sprinkle nuts on top of cake.

Pizzelle

Italian Cookie – A Family Christmas Tradition

Ingredients:

3 eggs
3/4 cup melted margarine
3/4 cup sugar
1 1/2 cups flour
1 teaspoon baking powder
2 teaspoons vanilla
3 tablespoons milk
1 teaspoon anise extract
2 teaspoons anise seeds

1. Beat eggs at high speed.
2. Melt margarine.
3. Mix butter; sugar; flour; baking powder; vanilla, milk; anise extract and anise seeds.
4. Preheat pizzelle iron and place 1 small spoonful of batter on the center of design.
5. Close lid for 1 to 2 minutes and remove with a fork.
6. Place on paper towel to cool.
7. Store in an air tight container with paper towels on top of pizzelles.

Pumpkin Bread

Ingredients:
1 cup canola oil
4 eggs
3 1/2 cups flour
1 teaspoon nutmeg
1 teaspoon cinnamon
1 teaspoon
2 teaspoons baking soda
3 cups sugar
2 cups pumpkin
1 cup walnuts
2/3 cup water

1. In a bowl combine flour; eggs; water and oil.
2. Add nutmeg and cinnamon.
3. Add baking soda and salt.
4. Add sugar; nuts and pumpkin.
5. Beat on low speed until well blended.
6. Grease 3 small loaf pans and line with waxed paper.
7. Pour batter equally into pans.
8. Bake in pre-heated oven at 350 degrees for 1 hour (check with a toothpick) to make sure cake is fully cooked.
9. Let cool for 20 minutes.

Pumpkin Lemon Pie

Carrillo Thanksgiving Tradition

Ingredients:

1 medium Mexican pumpkin
(green hard skin)
2 cups white sugar
½ gallon fresh milk
2 cups water
Pinch of salt
1 dozen eggs
1 bottle lemon extract
2 cups coconut

1. Fill a large pot of water and bring to a boil.

2. Cut pumpkin into 4-inch square pieces.

3. Place pumpkin with the skin in boiling water and cook until soft.

4. Drain water and remove pumpkin from skin.

5. Boil 2 cups water with 4 cups sugar for the syrup.

6. Pour syrup into the pumpkin and cook for 1 hour.

7. Beat together egg yolks and milk.

8. Beat egg whites and add sugar.

9. Blend in egg yolk mixture and lemon extract.

10. Blend mixture into pumpkin until it thickens and pour into pie shell.

11. Bake in pre-heated oven at 350 degrees for 40 minutes; add coconut; bake for 5 minutes.

Pie Crust

Ingredients:
1/2 cup flour
1/4 teaspoon baking powder
1/4 teaspoon salt
1/2 cup margarine (room temperature)
Ice water

1. In a medium bowl combine flour; baking powder and salt.
2. Add margarine.
3. Add ice water as needed to knead dough.
4. Shape dough in ball and chill for 1 hour.
5. Roll out dough and place in a 9-inch pie pan.

Rice Pudding

Ingredients:

2 cups long grain rice
1 cup dark raisins
1 can evaporated milk
1 pint whipping cream
1 tablespoon vanilla
1/2 cup sugar or to taste
3 cups water or to cover rice

1. In a medium pot cook rice with water to cover.

2. After rice has absorbed the water add; milk and stir.

3. Add vanilla; cinnamon and stir.

4. Add sugar to taste.

5. Whip 1 pint of whipping cream and fold into rice mixture.

6. Serve hot or cold.

Ritz Cracker Delight

Ingredients:
3 stiff egg whites
1 cup sugar
22 crushed Ritz crackers
1 teaspoon vanilla
1 teaspoon vinegar
1 teaspoon baking powder
1/2 cup pecans
1 can of blueberry pie filling
  or your choice

1. In a medium bowl combine stiff egg whites; sugar; crackers; vanilla; vinegar; baking powder and nuts.

2. Spread mixture in a 9-inch cake pan and bake at 350 degrees for 20 minutes.

3. Spread filling on cooled crust and top with frosting mixture.

Frosting

Ingredients:
1/2 pint whipping cream, whipped
1/4 cup sugar,
1/2 teaspoon vanilla
1 (8-ounce) package cream cheese

1. In a medium bowl beat whipping cream until it starts to stiffen.

2. Add sugar.

3. Add vanilla.

4. Add cream cheese.

5. Whipped ingredients until it turns to a frosting consistency.

Sopapias

Similar to Fry Bread

Ingredients:
2 cups flour
1/4 cup powdered milk
1 teaspoon salt
2 teaspoons baking powder
1 tablespoon lard or
    shortening
3/4 cup warm water
Honey or powdered sugar
    and cinnamon

1. In medium bowl mix flour; dry milk; baking powder and salt.

2. Mix in lard or shortening.

3. Add warm water as needed to knead dough.

4. Shape dough into 8 balls.

5. Roll out in small circles.

6. Let rise 10 minutes.

7. Fry in 400 degree oil for 1 to 2 minutes or until golden brown.

8. Drain oil on a loaf pan lined with paper towels.

9. Sprinkle with honey or cinnamon and sugar.

Sticky Buns

Ingredients:

1 package 22 frozen bread
   dough balls
1/2 cup margarine
1/2 cup brown sugar
1 teaspoon cinnamon
2 cups diced pecans
1 small box butterscotch
   instant pudding

1. In a greased bundt pan sprinkle pecans.
2. Place 18 to 20 defrosted balls of dough in bundt pan.
3. Sprinkle pudding on top of dough.
4. Melt margarine; add brown sugar and cinnamon.
5. Pour mixture on top.
6. Bake in pre-heated oven at 350 degrees for 25 minutes.

Viscochuelos

(Cookies) A Family Christmas Tradition

Ingredients:
2 cups flour
2/3 cup shortening
1/2 cups sugar
1/4 cup yellow corn meal
1/4 tablespoon salt
2 eggs
1 teaspoon warm water
2 teaspoons liquid anise
2 teaspoons anise seed
1 teaspoon vanilla

1. In a medium size bowl combine flour; shortening and sugar.
2. Add corn meal.
3. Add salt.
4. Add eggs.
5. Add water.
6. Add vanilla; liquid anise and seeds.
7. Mix dough until well blended.
8. Roll dough into 5-inch long worm shape and criss-cross into a ribbon.
9. Bake in preheated oven at 350 degrees until golden brown.

Waldorf Red Cake

Ingredients:
1 1/2 cups butter
1 1/2 cups sugar
2 eggs
2 ounces red food color
2 teaspoons cocoa
1 cup buttermilk
2 1/2 cups cake flour
1 teaspoon baking soda
1 teaspoon vinegar
1 teaspoon salt
1 teaspoon vanilla

1. In a medium size bowl cream butter; sugar and eggs.
2. Make a past out of cocoa and food coloring.
3. Add salt; buttermilk and mix.
4. Add flour and vanilla and mix.
5. Add baking soda and vinegar and mix well.
6. Pour mixture into two 3-inch x 8-inch greased pans lined with waxed paper.
7. Bake in pre-heated oven at 350 degrees for 30 minutes and let cool.
8. Spread frosting on cake.

Frosting

Ingredients:
3 tablespoons flour
1 cup milk
1 cup butter
1 cup sugar
1 teaspoon vanilla

1. Cook flour and milk until it thickens; let cool in fridge for 10 minutes.
2. Cream butter; sugar and vanilla.
3. Blend with cool mixture.

Zucchini Bread

Ingredients:
3 eggs
1 cup canola oil
2 cups sugar
2 cups grated zucchini
3 cups flour
1/3 teaspoon margarine
1 teaspoon baking soda
1/2 teaspoon baking powder
1 teaspoon cinnamon
1 teaspoon nutmeg
1 teaspoon vanilla
1/2 cups raisins
1/2 cup walnuts
1 cup shredded coconut

1. In a medium size bowl beat eggs, sugar and oil.
2. Add flour; baking soda; cinnamon; nutmeg and baking powder.
3. Add margarine; vanilla; raisins; zucchini; nuts and coconut and mix.
4. Pour mixture into 2 well greased loaf pans lined with waxed paper.
5. Bake in pre-heated oven at 350 degrees for 1 hour.

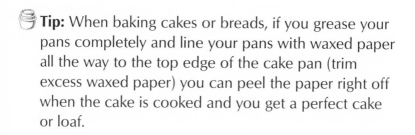 **Tip:** When baking cakes or breads, if you grease your pans completely and line your pans with waxed paper all the way to the top edge of the cake pan (trim excess waxed paper) you can peel the paper right off when the cake is cooked and you get a perfect cake or loaf.

Appetizers & Dips

Fresh Guacamole

Ingredients:
4 ripe avocados
2 diced jalapenos
2 tablespoons jalapeno juice;
    if needed
1 diced Roma tomato
1/2 cup diced green onion
1/2 cup chopped cilantro
Salt/pepper/garlic salt to taste

1. Scoop out avocado from skin and place in a small bowl and mash.
2. Add green onion; tomato and cilantro.
3. Add jalapenos.
4. Add juice if needed for a spiced up flavor.
5. Season with salt/pepper/ garlic salt to taste.
6. Mix until well blended.

Guacamole/Cottage Cheese Dip

Ingredients:
4 ripe avocados
1 pint cottage cheese
1 can diced green chili
Salt/pepper/garlic salt to taste

1. Scoop out avocado from skin and place in a small bowl and mash.
2. Add cottage cheese.
3. Add green chili.
4. Season with salt/pepper/ garlic salt to taste.
5. Mix until well blended.

 **Tip:** For a hotter flavor add 1 diced Jalapeno.

A Taste of Love from the Heart

Hot Sausage Cheese Balls

Ingredients:
1/2 pound hot sausage
1 cup finely shredded
　　Longhorn cheese
1 1/2 cups Bisquick

1. In small bowl combine sausage and cheese.
2. Add Bisquick and knead well.
3. Roll into balls and place on a cookie sheet.
4. Bake in pre-heated oven at 350 degrees for 20 minutes.

Jalapeno Dip

Ingredients:
1 large (8-ounce) package
　　cream cheese
1/2 green onion chives
1 teaspoon mayonnaise
2 tablespoons sour cream
1 teaspoon yellow mustard
　　sauce
3 drops Worchester sauce
1/2 cup dices jalapenos
3 tablespoons of jalapeno
　　juice
Salt/garlic salt/onion salt to
　　taste

1. In small bowl combine cream cheese and onion chives.
2. Add mayonnaise and sour cream.
3. Add mustard and Worchester sauce.
4. Add jalapenos and juice.
5. Season with salt/garlic salt/onion salt to taste.
6. Mix vigorously until well blended.

A Taste of Love from the Heart

Shrimp Dip

Ingredients:
1 pint sour cream
1 pint cottage cheese
1 small can baby shrimp
1 diced avocado
1/2 cup diced red bell
    pepper
1/2 cup diced green onion
1 diced jalapeno
Salt/pepper to taste

1. In small bowl combine sour cream and cottage cheese.
2. Add shrimp.
3. Add avocado.
4. Add bell pepper.
5. Add green onion.
6. Add jalapeno.
7. Mix well; salt/pepper to taste.

Sweet & Sour Meatballs

Ingredients:
3 cups pre-cooked meat balls
1/2 cup crushed pineapple
1 cup honey
1 cup barbeque sauce

1. In medium bowl combine meatballs with barbeque sauce.
2. Add pineapple.
3. Add honey and stir well.
4. Cover with paper towel.
5. Place in microwave for 4 minutes at 50% temperature.

Swedish Meatballs

Ingredients:
1 pound lean ground beef
1/2 pound lean ground pork
1/2 cup diced onion
3/4 cup dry bread crumbs
1 tablespoon fresh parsley
2 teaspoons salt
1/4 teaspoon pepper
1 teaspoon Worchester sauce
1 egg
1/2 cup milk
1/4 salad oil

1. In medium bowl combine beef; pork; onion; bread crumbs; parsley; salt; pepper Worchester sauce; egg and milk.

2. Mix well and refrigerate for 1 hour.

3. Roll 1 tablespoon of mixture into small balls.

4. In a large skillet heat oil and brown meatballs evenly until cooked.

Sauce

Ingredients:
1/4 cup flour
1 teaspoon paprika
1/2 teaspoon salt
1/8 teaspoon pepper
2 cups water
3/4 cup sour cream

1. In a skillet blend flour; paprika; salt and pepper.

2. Cook on low heat and stir until smooth and bubbly.

3. Add water and stir constantly to a boil.

4. Lower heat and add sour cream; mix until smooth.

5. Add meatballs to sauce.

A Taste of Love from the Heart

Velveeta Cheese Ball

A Family Christmas Tradition

Ingredients:

1 large box Velveeta cheese
2 large packages cream
   cheese
2 teaspoons finely diced
   garlic mashed
1 teaspoons Chili Tepines;
   mashed
Dried green parsley
Paprika

1. In medium bowl combine Velveeta and cream cheese.
2. Add garlic.
3. Add chili tepines.
4. Blend mixture until smooth.
5. Roll into ball or log shape.
6. Sprinkle heavily with parsley and paprika on waxed paper.
7. Roll the cheese shapes until all sides are covered.
8. Cover with aluminum foil and refrigerate for 2 hours; freezes well.

**Tip:** For added garlic flavor, you can use the juice from bottled garlic.

Water Chestnuts Wrapped in Bacon

Ingredients:
2 cans water chestnuts
1 pound bacon
1 small can pineapple juice
1 cup teriyaki sauce
Pointed toothpicks

1. Cut 1 pound bacon cut in half.

2. Wrap bacon strips around each chestnut and hold with a toothpick.

3. In a small saucepan add pineapple juice and teriyaki sauce and simmer on low heat for 1 minute.

4. Dip wrapped chestnuts in sauce.

5. Bake in pre-heated at 375 degrees until bacon cooks; approximately 10 minutes.

Notes

Drinks

Tropical Pineapple Delight

Ingredients:
1 (46-ounce) can of
     pineapple juice
1 (12-ounce) can lemonade
1 (12-ounce) can limeade
5 cups cold water
1 quart chilled club soda
Tequila (optional)

1. In a large punch bowl
   combine: water and
   pineapple juice.
2. Add lemonade and
   limeade.
3. Pour in club soda.
4. Add Tequila (optional).
5. Add ice and serve.

Champudo

Chocolate

Ingredients:
4 cone brown sugar
  (pilonzio)
2 quarts of water
2 cinnamon sticks
6 tablespoons cocoa
1/4 cup water
1 1/4 cups flour

1. In a medium pot boil 2 quarts water.

2. Add cone brown sugar and stir until dissolved.

3. Add cinnamon sticks.

4. Mix cocoa and water to make a paste.

5. Brown flour and put in a shaker (with wheel); add 1/2 cup water and shake vigorously.

6. Mix cocoa paste into boiling mixture and stir.

7. Add flour paste and stir until liquid thickens to a semi-thin consistency. You may need to thin or thicken mixture.

To my cousins, do you remember back in the years when winters were extremely cold and mom's had a pot of champudo boiling and hot gorditas right off the grill? I do! What a treat to dunk those gorditas into a cup dark chocolate champudo— those were the days!

A Taste of Love from the Heart

Hot Tate

Tea

Ingredients:
2 quarts of water
2 cinnamon sticks
1 cup raisins
2 large oranges, sliced
1 large lemon; sliced
1 cup sugar
1/2 cup rum
1/2 cup whiskey
1 tea bag

1. In a medium pot boil 2 quarts of water with tea bag.

2. Add cinnamon sticks.

3. Add sugar.

4. Add raisins.

5. Add orange slices.

6. Add lemon slices.

7. Stir continuously on low heat.

8. Add rum and whiskey; stir and continue heating for 10 minutes.

Orchata

Rice Water

Ingredients:
2 cups long grain rice
2 cups white sugar
1 teaspoon vanilla
3 cinnamon sticks
1 gallon water
6 cups ice cubes

1. In a blender grind rice until it's like fine powder.
2. Place rice powder in a gallon container and add water.
3. Add cinnamon sticks.
4. Add sugar to taste.
5. Add vanilla.
6. Add ice cubes; stir and cover.
7. Let sit in refrigerator over night.
8. Stir and run mixture through a strainer.
9. Serve ice cold.

Orchata is very soothing and yet refreshing drink. My children grew up drinking this beverage instead of sodas and Kool Aid. Rice water is very nourishing, so when my sons were sick with stomach situations, this helped to straighten out any type of intestinal problems. I now make this drink for the grandbabies and they also get the same pleasure from this drink. Many times children develop a milk allergy and are not able to digest dairy products, so the orchata seemed to do the trick in satisfying my grand-daughter.

Tom & Jerry (Nog)

Ingredients:
6 eggs
2 boxes powdered sugar
2 teaspoons vanilla
2 cans evaporated milk
2 cinnamon sticks
3 cups water
1 small carton whipping
    cream
1 ounce rum
1 ounce bourbon whiskey
Cinnamon
Nutmeg

1. Separate egg whites and beat on high until stiff.

2. Beat egg yolk and begin adding powdered sugar a little at a time.

3. Add vanilla and stir batter.

4. Beat whipping cream until it stiffens.

5. In medium size pot boil 3 cups water; add milk and cinnamon stick.

6. To serve place 1 tablespoon batter in each cup with milk mixture.

7. Add rum and bourbon to each cup and stir.

8. Sprinkle cinnamon and nutmeg on top and add whipping cream.

A Taste of Love from the Heart

Notes

Epilogue

Let me close by thanking all my readers for giving me the opportunity to be able to share with you, these recipes and history of my family. I am so grateful and fortunate to have you share my ventures and memories of traditions and food dishes that were passed down to me throughout the generations. May you share them with your loved ones and continue to pass them down throughout your generations.

To my sons and grandbabies, thank you for all the joy that you have brought into my heart. With the unconditional love and respect that you have given me, it bestowed the strength, confidence and the inner-spirit that I needed to endure through life. So my angels, I leave to you this legacy of your culture and heritage and always bear in mind, that my love for you will always be a truly divine love.

As I reflect back through my studies and life experiences, I have learned that the greatest gift that a human being can acquire in their life time is the gift of giving. Whether it be giving your heart, giving love, giving forgiveness, giving help, whatever the case may be, if it will assist or ameliorate another individual, then the end result is a priceless reward (you have also helped yourself). I invite you to put these words into practice and witness how your life will begin to flourish with happiness.

A Taste of Love from the Heart

And finally, I want to give tribute and adoration to the Lord. He has always been there to uplift me, encourage me and bless me. I praise him for giving me the knowledge, wisdom and the gift to write. Without the Lords help, I would never have been able to achieve and accomplish my goals that he has so inspired me to fulfill.